Beast
or Blessing

Stories and images about living with baboons in Africa

JENNI TRETHOWAN

Foreword by Allan Perrins

WITH A MESSAGE FROM DR JANE GOODALL

A Baboon Matters Trust Publication
PO Box 1776
Sun Valley
7985
Cape Town

Email baboonmatters@cybersmart.co.za
www.baboonmatters.org.za

First published in 2009

Publishing manager and designer: Belinda Ashton
www.thenatureconnection.co.za

Editor: Pat Brennan

Cover photographer: Lee Slabber – www.leeslabber.com

Illustrations: Daniel Clarke

Printed and bound by CTP Book Printers, Cape Town

ISBN 978-0-620-45772-9

Baboon *Matters*
Sustainable solutions *for managing baboons*

The Baboon Matters Trust raises awareness of the plight of baboons in southern Africa and facilitates the rescue and rehabilitation of baboons in need.

www.baboonmatters.org.za

Lee Slabber

To George Baboon, whose presence has enriched my life immeasurably

Chris Cole

Contents

Brett Cole

A MESSAGE from Dr Jane Goodall

Olive baboons share the habitat with the chimpanzees of Gombe National Park in Tanzania. They are far more numerous than the chimpanzees, and much less shy. On my very first day in Gombe I climbed a little way up the forested slope above my camp and, as I sat in a small clearing absorbing the atmosphere, was startled by loud barking – and there was a small group of baboons staring at me, barking and shaking branches. A big male yawned impressively, flashing his white eyelids and exposing his huge canines in a threat display.

We began studying the Gombe baboons in 1966. They are endlessly fascinating and over the years we have collected case histories and family histories, the transfers of males from one troop to another, the battles for dominance, the occasional infanticide or inter-community conflict. There is always something going on in a troop, especially when there are new babies around. The babies in their black coats are irresistible to other females who cluster round the mother, wanting to touch or groom – or even steal – the new arrival. There are always older children playing, chasing each other through the trees. You can see adult males sprawled with eyes closed as females groom them, searching through their thick coats. Others are feeding, digging in the ground for roots, or feasting on fruit up in the trees. When they are on the beach the juveniles may swim if the water is calm. The dominant male is so impressive, looking somehow arrogant with his thick mane and noble mein.

Unlike the chimpanzees, who are conservative in their tastes and have no wish to experiment with introduced human food, baboons are the ultimate opportunists. From the very start they invaded our tents, and nothing edible was safe unless it was secure inside a closed container. We could never eat if there were baboons anywhere nearby – and were just grateful that they went off to roost in their sleeping trees at dusk so that we could at least eat supper around the camp fire in peace. Things improved when we got our first buildings; but even so the baboons often managed to get in. Woe betide anyone who left the door unlatched if there were baboons nearby. And once inside, any food lying around was acceptable.

It is the baboon's adventurous and opportunistic spirit that causes so much conflict between baboon beings and human beings in places where there is overlap between human habitation and farmland, and the natural habitat of a baboon troop. They are so good at raiding crops which means that farmers hate them and resort to shooting them or trying to scare them off in other – often very cruel – ways. In some places, the women, out working in the fields, become terrified by the proximity of baboons. Indeed, they can be truly intimidating. Once I was surrounded by a circle of angry baboons, all threatening me – an infant was dying, and though it was nothing to do with me, I was a convenient scapegoat on whom the males could vent their concern and frustration.

I don't think I have ever been more terrified as, one after the other, the big males gave the yawn threat. They are formidable weapons, those teeth.

Unfortunately baboons are not the only other-than-human beings who come into conflict with us. In Asia it is some of the macaque species who occupy a similar niche to that of the baboon, and cause similar problems. And these problems, whether in Africa or Asia, are increasing all the time as the human population grows and relentlessly, bit by bit, moves into wilderness homes of other-than-human beings. It is we humans, not the monkeys, who create the problems. Not only do we move into monkey territory, but when monkeys have access to human food — mostly from farm land, but also from food thrown out or even fed to them — their population starts to increase, sometimes dramatically. And this makes the conflict ever more dire.

In Hong Kong, the Jane Goodall Institute, through its Roots & Shoots programme for young people, initiated a project whereby national parks staff trained high school volunteers as Monkey Ambassadors. They went from house to house in problem areas talking about monkey behaviour and giving tips on how to avoid confrontations. A similar program was very effective in Singapore. And I love the project initiated by one of our Roots & Shoots youth leaders in a small Tanzanian village. In retaliation for crop raiding, farmers were setting fire to the one remaining patch of forest where the baboons lived — thus making them increasingly likely to raid the fields. A group of primary school children learned about baboon behaviour, their rich social life, and the bonds between family members.

These children then went to talk to the farmers and helped to guard the crops. And they also collected seeds from the wild foods the baboons ate, and planted them in the forest to increase the natural food supply.

When I met Jenni Trethowan, the 'Baboon Lady', I was impressed by her absolute commitment to, and affection for, the baboons of Table Mountain. They could not, surely, have a more passionate advocate — and she has the full support of her family and a group of people who care, friends of the baboons. Together they are doing so much to help both baboons and people.

Beast or Blessing is timely. More and more people are becoming involved in the conflicts between ourselves and our simian relatives. The first major conference has been organized to bring such people together to discuss the problems and search for solutions as Jenni has done throughout this book.

Indeed, *Beast or Blessing*, with its sometimes moving, sometimes heart wrenching and sometimes very funny stories, will go a long way to helping people understand the problems and help us to find solutions.

My warmest good wishes are with you, Jenni, and your followers, and with the baboons to whom you have devoted so much of your energy, passion and love.

Jane Goodall

Jane Goodall Ph.D., DBE
Founder – the Jane Goodall Institute &
UN Messenger of Peace
www.janegoodall.org

FOREWORD *by Allan Perrins*

'Love them or hate them', baboons are an indispensable part of a susceptible eco-system that has earned the Cape recognition as one of the 'Floral Kingdoms of the World' and this alone must account for their conservation-worthy status.

Unfortunately, whereas some have grown to admire the complex social groupings and intelligence of baboons, others, sadly, argue that they are a potentially dangerous inconvenience, an impediment to development and that they should rather be exterminated or relocated.

Regrettably during 2009, levels of intolerance escalated into war-like proportions (both in and outside of the boardroom) and just as in the early 1990s, when the authorities decided to trap and mercilessly kill an entire troop of Kommetjie baboons for no apparent good reason, they once again appear to be at a complete loss as to how to deal with so-called 'problem baboons' without having to reach for the gun.

I took the decision to add my voice and influence to the appeal for sense and reason to prevail back in the '90s, and I continue today to be a strong advocate for this much-maligned species.

Peaceful co-existence need not be achieved through the barrel of a gun and it's never too late to educate the ignorant or change perceptions.

Baboons are capable of expressing and eliciting a wide range of human-like emotions from laughter to tears and are adept to an ever-changing environment, which is why they have survived against seemingly insurmountable odds. We should all be wary of the dreadful consequences of a landscape devoid of baboons and fight to preserve them from extinction, which unfortunately is one thing that we humans have perfected.

I personally owe the animals in my life, including the baboons, a debt of gratitude for causing me to see the relevance and significance of all of God's creatures. The honour and privilege of leading the oldest and largest SPCA in Africa is no mere coincidence. It is providence and I am proud to be an advocate for the protection and conservation of all animals – a priceless gift that I would be remiss to ever take for granted.

I salute and admire Jenni's dedicated work to protect our baboons and I hope that after paging through this beautiful book, you will have a greater insight into this fascinating species and join me and so many others in fighting for their protection.

Allan Perrins is CEO Cape of Good Hope SPCA

My work with baboons

It was a warm winter morning, one of those perfect Cape days where the air is clear, the sun a delight and the wind is still. A distant stream tumbled down the mountain adding a soothing melody to the swish of restios and grasses as they swayed in a wisp of breeze. Around me the baboons relaxed. Taking a welcome break from the rain and cold they lazed on rocks, grooming each other half-heartedly or just basking, absorbing every bit of warmth they could.

The rich smell of baboons, the occasional grunt between family members, a contented sigh – or raucous fart – the familiar sounds of the troop all added to my sense of contentment. Eric, the old man of the mountain and living legend, stretched his tired old body and, opening one eye, looked straight at me, acknowledging 'you again'. Then, settling into a more comfortable position, he drifted back to sleep. I glanced to my left towards Eric's son Anele and found myself gazing into the bright golden and mischievous eyes of this young male. His look was full of humour, but he was also watching out for his old father. Anele flopped down on his back, grabbed his feet in his hands and looked over to see what I thought of that; then closed his eyes and went to sleep – he didn't really worry what I thought at all.

As I sat on the mountain, I was overcome by a sense of timelessness: everything was as it was, as it should be – as it could be.

Away from the houses, away from the roads and noisy urban edge, it was easy to be lulled into a false sense of well-being. Baboons have been roaming the southern peninsula for tens of thousands of years,

possibly longer. They should be at peace here, this is their home. But with primates, peace is a fragile thing; and between baboons and humans I wonder if it is achievable at all.

Throughout southern Africa there have always been baboons; our various cultures are full of stories and songs about them. The folklore, rock art and modern art show the complete polarisation of opinion and attitudes that typifies baboons. Love them or hate them – very few people are ambivalent when it comes to baboons.

I started working with baboons in 1990, when an entire troop of baboons was exterminated in my home village of Kommetjie. The reason for this elimination? A few residents had complained, and, at that time, this was the way the authorities dealt with problem animals.

Sometimes you do need a catalyst for change. The elimination of the Kommetjie troop was that catalyst. Together with a small group of committed and determined people, I started the Kommetjie Environmental Awareness Group (KEAG). Our goal was to encourage a different approach to

dealing with baboons: management rather than elimination.

I have been working with baboon-related issues since then, and over the years I have noticed that no matter which village, farm or province I go to, people say "Our baboons are the smartest, strongest baboons". Although many times the statement is made in anger, I cannot help noticing that there is also an element of reluctant pride amongst the frustration.

The range of emotions engendered by baboons is huge – from the most basic rage through to absolute fascination – and from this wide range of emotions comes a wealth of stories. Over the past twenty years I have gained a certain notoriety as the 'baboon lady', and everywhere I go people have their own special baboon stories to tell me.

I thought that it would be a great idea to gather some of these stories together and thanks to the support of Mosa Le Roux and the Nussbaum Foundation, the Baboon Matters Trust is able to publish a collection of your best baboon stories.

Baboons have roamed southern Africa for many thousands of years and today remnant populations of these fascinating primates live precariously alongside us in an ever-changing world.

Chris Cole

The most beautiful of apes is hideous in comparison to man, and the wisest of men is an ape before God — **Plato**

Chapter One

Baboons through the ages

'Baboons got here first' is one of the most oft-repeated slogans of the 'pro-baboon brigade' – a statement that infuriates the 'anti-baboons'. But facts are facts, baboons have been here in southern Africa for at least two million years. A quick glance at baboon history proves this point, however moot the point may be.

15 million years ago – In 1997 fossils of old world monkeys (the taxonomic category into which baboons fall) were discovered in Africa. These fossils date back 15 million years.

Four million years ago – The baboons we see today belong to a taxonomic group (genus) called *Papio*. Based on fossil and genetic evidence, baboons originated in southern Africa about four million years ago, then gradually spread out to most of sub-Saharan Africa. By comparison, our genus *Homo* is about two million years old, but our modern ancestors date back only about 200 000 years.

Two thousand years ago – We know that ancient Egyptians worshipped baboons. The Hamadryas baboons, a species of baboon found in northern Africa, were thought to represent Thoth, the god of wisdom, and there are depictions of four sacred baboons worshipping the sun in the temple to Thoth at Hemmopolis.

In addition to being worshipped in temples, baboons appear in many hieroglyphics; they are seen with what appear to be leads and it is thought that many households kept baboons as family pets.

The last few hundred years – Closer to home, baboons have been found in rock art dating back hundreds of years and certainly feature in the ancient tales of Africa. The story below of Cagn (the equivalent of God or Creator in Bushman folklore) and the baboons reflects how people and animals start to move away from common goals.

Long ago, baboons were little men like the Bushmen, but mischievous and quarrelsome. One day they met Cagn's son, Cogaz, who had been sent by his father into the bush to collect sticks to make bows. 'Oh ho!' they jeered, dancing around the boy, 'Your father thinks he is so clever, making bows to kill us. We will kill you instead.' So they killed poor Cogaz and tied him up in the top of a tree, and danced around it singing in their own tongue, 'Cagn thinks he is clever!' Soon Cagn, who was asleep, awoke and sensed that there was something wrong. He called to his wife Coti to bring him his charms. He rubbed some magic on his nose and thought and thought. Then up he jumped. 'The little men have hanged Cogaz,' he said and off he went to where they were dancing. When they saw him coming they were frightened and changed their chant, but a little girl said, 'Don't sing that way, sing it the way you were singing before.' And Cagn ordered, 'Sing as the little girl wishes,' and they were obliged to sing and dance as before. So Cagn said, 'Yes! That is the song I heard, that is what I wanted; go on dancing until I return.' He went and fetched a basket full of pegs and went behind each of them as they danced, making a great deal of dust, and drove a peg into each one's backside with a crack. They all bounded off to the mountains, barking and leaping with their baboon tails sticking up behind, to live on roots, beetles and scorpions and to scratch fleas and chatter nonsense forever. Then Cagn climbed up into the tree and took down Cogaz and by magic restored him to life.

It is a fact that to this day Bushmen seem to be the only people that not only understand the language of the baboons but to a limited extent can even converse with them. (from Kiki Amedja website)

Lee Slabber

The adaptation of another African folk tale sent to me by **Christine Riley** illustrates how people acknowledge the cunning of baboons, and try to take advantage –

"In parts of Africa where droughts are common, locations of waterholes become a secret, and it is thought that baboons will only go to them when they are sure that no-one is looking. Hunters devised a method of finding these secret waterholes. A hunter will approach a group of baboons, dig a small hole in an embankment and place some fruit in it. The hole is just big enough for the baboon to reach in but too small to withdraw if its fist is closed. Once the baboon reaches in and grabs the fruit, releasing is not an option. It will shriek as the hunter approaches and struggle to escape, but it just will not let go of the fruit. The hunter collars the animal, ties it to a post, feeds it some salt to induce thirst and then lets it sit for a couple of days without water. As soon as it is released, the baboon wastes no time running to the waterhole, and the hunter follows it to the water…"

In my years of working with baboons and in baboon-related matters, it has been difficult to work out what the majority opinion on baboons actually is – the issue is so exceptionally polarised that no single view-point can be agreed as the accepted norm. Some ancient African stories illustrate how far back the polarisation goes – from the ancient Egyptians who worshipped baboons and even kept them as treasured household pets, to the Bushmen who chastised and punished them.

In his book 'African Folktales in the New World', William Russell Bascom theorises that baboons are often portrayed as the dupes of the animal world – not cunning creatures at all. I have taken the liberty of condensing the tale that Bascom uses to demonstrate his point.

It was a time of great drought, and because he was so hungry Hare stole and ate all of Lion's cubs. Lion was furious and intent on punishing the animal that had done such a dreadful thing. Hare realised that if found out, he would be in terrible trouble, so when he saw vain Baboon sitting in the sun grooming, he made a devious plan to shift the blame. Hare wove an elaborate tale – resulting in Baboon demanding to know the words of a 'secret' song. So Hare 'reluctantly' taught Baboon the words – "I ate Lion's cubs, I ate Lion's cubs". Once Hare had set up the Baboon, he hid Lion in a bundle of grass, then got Baboon to sing his new song – when Lion heard the song he leapt out of his hiding place, killing all the innocent baboons and Hare got off scot-free…

What is interesting about this tale is that it has been told in several slightly differing variations over most of Africa. From the range of this particular story – Nigeria through to Mozambique and South Africa – it seems that in African folklore baboons were seen to be vain and gullible, rather than clever.

In Europe baboons and apes were making their presence felt as early as the Middle Ages when their close resemblance to humans was cause for huge consternation – earning them the tag 'Spirit Diablo' – meaning spirit of the devil. The reason for the bad image was as much to do with the humans who introduced the apes to Europe as it was to do with the cunning of the primates themselves.

Frequently it was travelers who encountered apes on their journeys, so it was often gypsies or disreputable seamen who introduced monkeys and occasionally baboons to Europe.

The classic image of the organ grinders with monkeys in costume were the first contact many European villagers had with the amazing apes – but carefully trained primates pick-pocketing unsuspecting audiences at travelling side shows certainly did much to create the illusion of devil incarnate.

In 1573 the poet Thomas Weelkes wrote a poem illustrating the difference between species of primates. Sadly baboons do not come off well.

The Ape, the Monkey and Baboon

The ape, the monkey and baboon did meet
And breaking of their fast in Friday street,
Two of them swore together solemnly
In their three natures was a sympathy.

Nay, quoth baboon,
I do deny that strain,
I have more knavery in me
Than you twain.

Why, quoth the ape, I have a horse at will
In Paris Garden for to ride on still,
And there show tricks. Tush, quoth the monkey,
For better tricks in great men's houses lie.

Tush, quoth baboon,
When men do know I come,
For sport from city, country
they will run.

Jenni Trethowan

It would take too long to go through the entire history of baboons, so I have skipped ahead to this newspaper headline from 1933 which shows a certain sense of sympathy, even sadness, at the plight of the baboons –

By the 1950s there was a wry humour and almost acceptance of baboons in the South Peninsula –

VISITORS JUMPED —BUT BABOONS?

By a Staff Reporter

AN anti-baboon scare-gun was hoisted to its post at Cape Point yesterday and sent ear-splitting blasts reverberating through baboon country near the parking area.

Visitors to the nature reserve jumped apprehensively at each explosion, while from the bush baboons watched unseen.

'I know they are there,' said the warden of the reserve (Mr. Godfrey Baynes), 'but they will not show themselves while I am here in my uniform.'

The scare-gun explodes its water and carbide mixture every two minutes for 12 hours. Mr. Baynes hopes it will frighten away baboons which have been making food-hunting forays on unguarded cars at the parking area.

The noise is startling and can be heard hundreds of yards away. But some Cape Pointers believe it will frighten picnickers more than the baboons who will get used to the gun in time and will continue to approach visitors who encourage their presence by feeding.

There is no evidence yet of the gun on the baboons. But since the post for the gun was erected a week ago the animals have kept away from the parking area.

'I am not surprised. The post resembles a gibbet, and sent a shiver down my spine as I looked at it starkly outlined against the False Bay skyline.'

The gun operated for a short while yesterday afternoon. Workmen took it down from the post before nightfall.

'If we leave it here the baboons will probably take it away,' said one of the men.

WARDEN of the Cape Point Nature Reserve (Mr. Godfrey Baynes) looks enamoured of the prospect of an ear-splitting explosion from the anti-baboon gun above his head.

APRIL 25, 1933
CAPE TIMES, TUES
VAIN FIGHT FOR EXISTENCE
THE PENINSULA'S EXILED TRIBE OF BABOONS
DOOM OF ULTIMATE EXTINCTION
STORY OF ITS DEPOSED LEADER
GORY COMBATS WITH "MR. BLIKKIE"

Some Were Amused

Inquisitive baboons amused some visitors to the Cape Point Nature Reserve at the Easter week-end and terrified others. These pictures were taken on Sunday. One of the baboons clambered into an unguarded car and handed out sandwiches and apples to other baboons outside. It struck a woman who tried to open a door of the car. Another baboon badly scared a young girl by catching hold of her skirts.

Cape Times 21/4/50.

Far from resolving or shedding light on why there is conflict between man and baboons, all my research into the history of baboons indicates thus far, is that baboons have in fact been around for millions of years, and sadly the conflict has been around for a very long time – with polarity stalking every step of the journey between primates.

The baboon as archetypal messenger

by Prof. Graham Saayman, author of Hunting with the Heart

The Ancient Egyptians considered the baboon a sacred animal worthy of mummification. The deep-chested bark of the troop leaders, echoing over the krantzes and across the valleys just before first light, is a wonderful welcome to the sun and an invitation to the day. Those who built the pyramids venerated the farsighted baboon as the one who signifies daily rebirth after the soul has descended into the darkening sea of night.

Baboons still subsist on Table Mountain and they survive throughout southern Africa, their distribution limited by the availability of safe sleeping sites. The clowns and fools of myths and folklore, in the old days the Zulu people fed them in time of drought. But in modern times animals, both great and small, have been tamed, domesticated, televised and demystified, their habitat denuded, their potency absorbed, their energy cannibalised.

The modern age has failed to treat Nature with compassion: forests denuded to feed the forges and machinery of materialism, dead zones of pollution across the oceans, escalating climate change, the window of hope closing as the human species lurches closer to extinction.

In this depressing scenario, the baboon is central to the contemporary controversy about the natural order, the web of life and ethical considerations here in the Cape where the great herds of animals were shot out long ago during the colonial conquest.

The baboon has great psychological significance as the mercurial Trickster figure in African mythology and folklore. In times of adversity the baboon invites us to look at the bright side and to activate our sense of humour when the going gets tough. The baboon also reflects the dark side of the human psyche and suggests the necessity to accept personal ethical responsibility at times of interpersonal crisis or conflicts of interest.

Somewhat paradoxically, modern civilization, obsessed by the conquest of nature, has arrived at terracide as a likely outcome of tinkering with technology. Distinguished earth scientists predicted long ago that manmade global warming, a side effect of science and industrial pollution, would produce effects as devastating as full-scale nuclear war. Ecological impacts, rather than politics, are likely to shape the future of the human race.

The vanishing polar bear stalks the human family's dreams. And when the last barks of baboons echo and recede over the krantzes of the Cape, the world will be a sadder and a more perilous place.

The modern collective has yet to learn that if there's no room in the world for Wilderness, then there's no room in the world for us.

It is mysterious if a baboon falls from a tree
Shona Proverb

Chapter Two

In search of an easy meal

Some of the stories from African folklore depict baboons as cunning and adaptable, while others depict baboons as vain and lazy, but none of the stories I could find demonstrated the hatred and anger that frequently typify modern-day encounters with baboons. So when and why did it all change and why is the conflict so often with baboons rather than other apes?

The answer lies partly in the choice of habitat: the great apes stick mainly to the forest areas, by definition areas not ideally suited to large-scale farming. Baboons, however, are more inclined to habitats where farming is viable, and so the conflict between people and baboon can realistically be traced back to the time when we started to farm.

We all know just how adaptable baboons are, and so it is easy to imagine the cunning baboon sitting in nearby trees watching a farmer hard at work preparing and then planting his crops. Nonchalant baboon then weighs up the exact moment to sneak down and steal the results of all that labour — it is not difficult to imagine just how angry this would make the hard-working farmer!

In some African cultures the farmers anticipated raids from baboons and some of the bird species. In anticipation of these raids, certain taboos were initiated and crops were planted to co-ordinate natural fruiting cycles of indigenous trees with the planting of crops. In Zimbabwe, for example, the planting of maize coincided with the fruiting of loquat trees. It was considered taboo for farmers to pick the loquat fruit, because if they did the baboons would come and raid the young maize crops. (from Jacob Mapara – 'Indigenous Knowledge Systems in Zimbabwe Juxtaposing Postcolonial Theory').

In Cape Town, the first white settlers were determined to set up productive market gardens for the East Indies shipping route, and there are diary entries detailing how baboons stole from these industrious farmers in the late 1600s. For many years the situation between humans and baboons reached an uneasy peace in the Mother City, mainly a result of the bounty placed on so-called 'problem animals'.

From the arrival of the Dutch East Africa Trading Company settlers in 1652 until 1862, when the last lion was shot in what is now Mowbray, there was an unprecedented slaughter of wildlife, so that today the baboon is the last large mammal to be found outside of national parks. The impact of this notion of 'problem animals' or 'vermin species' has been enormous. Thousands of animals have been unjustly slaughtered, but even more abhorrent is the

resulting mindset — the way in which it became acceptable to consider animals as the problem, rather than our own impacts. Ironically, it is clear that this attitude has been unsuccessful. Despite the killing of many hundreds if not thousands of baboons, they have survived and the age-old problems remain unsolved.

We can see how the pieces of this conflict puzzle start to fall into place — baboons adapt quickly to getting easy food; humans start farming and the crops are seen by baboons as easy food. So for a long time the conflict between people and baboons was confined to the farming areas.

But baboons are above all else opportunists. They have an innate ability to weigh up the risks versus potential rewards and, if the rewards are high enough, the smart, adaptable baboon will take a few well-planned risks.

Many of the stories told to me involve baboons taking food from unsuspecting humans. Some of the humans reacted with anger and fear, but some retold their stories with amazement — and amusement.

Spaghetti, Avo and Banana

by David Rattle, Capri Village

My best meeting with a baboon occurred last year when a lone male from the Kommetjie troop, we think it may have been Spaghetti, went walk-about — looking for another troop to join. He landed up at our old farmhouse in Capri.

I was in the outside room that we call 'the office' when our housekeeper, Patricia, came skedaddling down the few stairs leading to the door, breathlessly whispering: "Mr Davie, Mr Davie, it's an animal, there's an animal!" I'm not sure how, but I knew immediately what the problem was — although it had never happened before — there was a baboon in the house.

We're very open plan and in the summer we have lots of doors open during the day. Apparently, he'd just suddenly appeared and come in, no problem. By the time I arrived at the front door, there he was facing me on the dining room table, sitting legs apart and casually plucking, peeling and eating bananas from a large bunch he'd helped himself to from the kitchen. Totally unconcerned, oblivious to the incompatibility of a wild animal in a sophisticated domestic interior — what a picture he made!

Truthfully, because I had learned much from stories of other encounters, I wasn't too worried. I knew I just needed to contain the situation and implement potential damage control. The dogs were dozing out on the stoep — clearly having absolutely no idea we had an intruder. So much for our watchdogs (actually two very old pavement specials, a male, Dingo, and a little feisty old female, Kwela). I quietly told Patricia, who was standing well behind me, "I'm going to call the dogs in. When they come, you shut them in the spare bedroom."

First in was Dingo. He let out a small woof of surprise, totally affronted at the sight of this intruder. But he walked stiffly past with as much dignity as he could muster. Affronted he may have been but he very definitely showed absolutely no desire to 'engage'. Kwela followed him in casually, took a very quick look and literally winced. I must say, I've never seen a dog do that before. Screwing up her eyes, she made a face as if she had just bitten into a lemon and, grimacing hideously, tiptoed past into the bedroom with considerable alacrity. Patricia closed the door. We both breathed a sigh of relief. Problem number one had been averted. Now all we had to do was to get Spaghetti out.

Patricia closed the front and main bedroom doors while I stood there talking soothingly to him. I saw my cell phone, also on the dining table, and I quietly reached for it. I don't think he was interested but there's a lot of it about these days and you can't be too careful. Now there was just the door to the stoep open to him and I started schmoosing him gently towards it, but by this time Spaghetti had finished his bunch of bananas and obviously had other ideas. He hopped down from the table and headed – not for the stoep door – but back to the kitchen. Oh dear, I hadn't anticipated this. But the French door in the kitchen was wide open so all was not lost. We followed him in, Patricia now closing the stoep door, and with relief we watched as he ambled through the French door, helping himself to another banana and an avocado on the way.

Suddenly I saw Eric the gardener at the garden shed with his lunchtime sandwiches – if he saw Spaghetti I knew he'd freak; but if Spaghetti smelled the sandwiches – oh no – this was a recipe for disaster! And I couldn't shout because I was less than three metres from you-know-who. In a flash of inspiration, I fast-dialled Eric on my cell phone. His phone rang and he went back inside the shed to answer it. He must have got the shock of his life when he heard: "Eric, this is Dave here. I want you to do exactly as I say. Turn around and close the door. Okay? Do you understand? I'm watching you."

Strangely enough, he did it! Then Patricia closed the kitchen door, and suddenly Spaghetti was out and the house was secure. Hallelujah! Now it was just him and me. Sitting nonchalantly on our wrought-iron table, he'd finished his last banana and was now peeling and tucking into his avocado.

I stood less than two metres away and as I talked to him I quietly dialled Annie on my cell phone. "Hi darling," I whispered, "you won't believe who I'm standing next to..."

But not for long. As soon as his avo was finished he deposited the skin and the stone (very neatly) on the table beside us and off he went, hopping over our neighbour's fence, in search of pastures new.

How lonely, just for a moment, I felt. And how privileged and how grateful, even now, do I feel to have been paid a visit by such a truly magnificent, wild but ever so gentle creature.

I remembered to let Eric out about half an hour later.

Lee Slabber

One story which I think has almost become an urban legend has been told to me by a number of different people from the small village where the incident took place. (I have been asked to keep the location a secret as the bakery has become very well-known in ensuing years.)

It seems that in this tiny seaside village a small home-style bakery was becoming increasingly successful and had to employ a number of local residents in order to meet a large pre-Christmas order. It was a hot summer's day and so the doors were all opened onto the garden. The workers were in a long production line, packaging rusks – time was of the essence and each person was intent on their specific task. After a while the 'end of line' person noticed that each packet was missing at least two rusks. Looking back up the line he was amazed to see a large male baboon calmly standing between two of his colleagues. As each open packet of rusks was passed down the production line, the baboon would take a couple of rusks and was frantically storing them in cheek pouches or under his arms.

When the workers all finally noticed the baboon, there was a panicked outcry and a frantic scramble to move away from the large male – who casually grabbed a few more rusks before running from the building on his legs, clutching rusks in his fists, and others tucked under his arms. A few paces from the building he stopped and sat in the sun and ate his mid-afternoon snack.

Lee Slabber

Chris Burlock sent the following anecdote from Rooi Els. This story is only hearsay, but I love it –

A woman was taking a tray of muffins from the oven, using oven-gloves, but when she turned around to place them on the counter behind her, two hairy hands reached out to take the tray from her!

But the baboon sitting on the counter did not have oven-gloves on and was forced to toss the tray into the air to relieve the burning. But reluctant to lose his meal, he kept catching it again! I'd have loved to see the juggling act for myself!

What is so important to remember about baboons is their inherently opportunistic nature. Once they have enjoyed an easy meal, they will almost certainly be back for another – and another, and after all who can blame them? What starts off as funny and poignant can easily become irritatingly impactful – and costly! Baboons can cause a huge amount of damage to property, crops and even your hard-won veggie patch!

So, amusing as these stories are, we need to remember our goal is to keep baboons on the mountains and away from the houses, and the best way to do that is to ensure the food is not easy to get at!

Chris Cole

Chapter Three

Waste not - want not

Over the years there have been more and more reports of damage done by baboons. Is the situation getting worse? Are baboons getting bolder and more aggressive? Is it only a matter of time until they kill someone?

A few more pieces of the conflict puzzle fall into place when we remember that baboons are opportunistic and, rather like us, will always try to find an easy option. Add to the puzzle the fact that human beings are taking up more and more space on the planet and now add one of the most important pieces of all – we humans are a wasteful species!

It has been estimated that two thirds of all food purchased ends up as waste. That is a staggering amount of food that is literally thrown away!

Around the world animals are adapting well to our wasteful habits. Whether it is bears or racoons in the USA, foxes in London, or baboons in Cape Town, there is a common thread: the animals are adapting more quickly to us than we are to them. These creatures have learnt that our garbage contains good things to eat.

The delightful film 'Over the Hedge' illustrates this concept wonderfully, as do some stories from local residents.

Brett Cole

An exceptional, exciting visit from the wild

by Brenda Gibbs, Constantia

At about 9h00 on a beautiful, hot autumn morning, I heard the sound of 'something' landing heavily on our bedroom roof, and thought, "Wow, that must be a big squirrel!"

Walking to our bedroom door and glancing down the passage towards the kitchen, I couldn't believe my eyes! There he was sitting in at the patio door! He looked as if he owned the place! He was truly magnificent! He was a big male baboon! Huge, about 30kgs and he had a beautiful coat. He was in prime condition, confident and so silent!

I quickly closed Louie, our Irish Terrier, in our bedroom, and gingerly made my way to the entrance hall phone to alert Peter, who was working upstairs.

Winnie, our char, was standing in the passage near me when the baboon came inside. She nearly fainted with fright, and in a flash, locked herself in the bathroom!

The baboon walked through the lounge, into the dining room and through the family room. When he got into the games room, he tipped over a bin looking for something to eat.

As he was returning through the dining room, Peter came down the stairs. The baboon saw him, did not alter the pace of his stride and sauntered through to the kitchen.

Thankfully, the baboon remembered how to find his way back into the entrance hall and to the only open door, the same door that he had used to enter our home. As effortlessly and silently as he entered, the baboon went out again!

It all happened so suddenly, such an unusual sight. We felt amazed by what we had seen. David's visit had lasted no longer than 15 minutes but we would remember it always.

All this time I was desperate to fetch my camera! Walking behind the baboon, yet keeping a safe distance, I only managed to reach the lounge when the baboon started to retrace his path! What a fabulous photo it would have been!

Luckily, the baboon did not feel scared or agitated or cornered during his visit. (Baboon's canines are larger than those of lions and they can give an awful bite if they are cornered.)

When he left, he walked across the patio, down the tennis court stairs to the corner of our plot, climbed up the tennis-court fence and jumped onto the neighbour's garage roof and disappeared.

Our first baboon visitor in 30 years! Fortunately for us he was on his own and not leading the troop!

From the barking made by the dogs further down the neighbourhood, we could guess the direction he was going in. He was making his way towards the green belt. We hoped that he would be safe.

It's wild in the city!

Sadly David baboon's story did not have a happy ending. He was captured in the Cape Town suburbs and was relocated to a nature reserve near to Du Toits Kloof. David was passing through a farm when the farm dogs chased him up a tree. The farmer cut the tree down – with David still in the tree – and the farm dogs tore the now-dazed baboon to pieces.

In another tale, ex-Kommetjie resident **Sarah Titley** relates waking to a rather 'odd noise'. On checking to find the source of the commotion she discovered a couple of juvenile baboons having a wonderful time rummaging through the waste in the garbage bin. The bin was rolling around as the juveniles fought over the tastier scraps while still inside the bin!

With the benefit of hindsight it is easy to see how the situation has deteriorated to this point. In years gone by, baboons were first attracted to the crops of farmers. Now with the rapid urban sprawl our towns and cities have made an impact on undeveloped areas so baboons notice the fruit trees, vegetables and edible plants, richly compacted into relatively small areas. As the baboons explore the gardens they notice fabulous receptacles with plenty of food, those trash bins are just so appealing! From the gardens it is easy to check through our big windows, seeing our glorious fruit bowls! Virtually every home has a fruit bowl and generally, we display those fruit bowls proudly and visibly on a table or counter top. Imagine, from the baboons' point of view, just what a feast we are laying out.

It is not difficult to see why baboons cautiously started venturing from the garden into our homes –

the rewards are high and tasty! A half loaf of bread is enough calorific requirement for the whole day – in simple terms if the baboons can get just half a loaf of bread they can take the rest of the day off. I know I can relate to that: if I could do all my work in a quick half hour of activity I would love to take the rest of the day off!

One of the trends I noticed from the many people who sent me their stories, was that the majority of incidents took place on weekends or public holidays – coincidence? Not really. If you think about it, it is on weekends or public holidays that many of us enjoy open houses, picnics or dining al fresco on the patio. It is precisely those times when the houses are open and we are relaxed that opportunities for watchful baboons abound.

Mrs J Portersmith of Simon's Town sent me a Christmas tale of a different sort –

It was December 2006, a week before Christmas. I had the family here on holiday. I had finished the washing when quietly behind me in came a big baboon. He jumped up onto the kitchen counter, grabbed two packets of potato crisps, sat there and ate them. I did not disturb him but immediately closed the interleading door and left him to enjoy his Christmas. Afterwards he left as quietly as he came, but left me to clean up the mess.

Meantime the Shekyls family of Welcome Glen also had a Christmas visitor…

Noskethi comes for Christmas dinner!

by the Shekyls Family, Welcome Glen

Armand, Melanie, Tylan and Keandra (my son, daughter-in-law and grandchildren) from Gauteng were, as usual, visiting with me for Christmas. They adore our baboons and can't wait for the baboons to make an appearance in our village! The children were very fortunate this time round, because a male named Noskethi had made himself at home on my property. Apparently he had been shot the previous March, and was recuperating from his horrific ordeal. December is one of our hottest months and Noskethi was always looking for a bit of shade to rest in and have a nap. He was aware that I do not have dogs and that I do not mind the baboons coming onto my property.

For about a week and a half, Noskethi would arrive in the morning, have a drink of water in the birdbath, and then climb onto the roof of the pergola outside the kitchen door. There he would sit a while, surveying his surroundings and then, after a huge yawn, would lie down for a nap and to rest his weary body. When the sun moved around the corner, beating down on where he was sleeping, he would climb down, go for a walk-about (to the disgust of the neighbourhood dogs) and then return for another drink of water. He then would climb onto the roof of the pergola on the front verandah,

to rest once more in the shade. We could come and go about our daily business and it did not bother him at all. Even the children playing in the garden did not disturb him!

One fine day the children had some GREAT excitement. The helicopters were collecting water from the sea in their huge buckets to douse a fire somewhere in the vicinity. After emptying the buckets, the helicopters came to land on the Navy sports field. They would pause a while and then take off again. The sports field is almost opposite my home and we had a lovely view from the front verandah. The children could not believe their eyes and were so engrossed in what was happening that they completely forgot about Noskethi. He, in the meantime, had moved from the kitchen pergola roof to the front veranda pergola roof. Once the helicopters had departed, we all came inside and closed (we thought) the front 'baboon' gate. The children carried on playing and I continued preparing supper.

Tylan and Keandra called me, very quietly, and said: "Look, Ouma," pointing at the front door. There was Noskethi, sitting and watching everything that was happening inside. The children were so glad that he had come down, and they sat inside of the baboon gate. They were talking to Noskethi and examining every detail of his face, hands and feet. They even noticed that he had a small cut on the pad of one of his feet. Happy that my grandchildren from Gauteng had such a wonderful privilege to interact with a baboon at such a close range, I went about preparing supper.

The next moment I heard a commotion, kids shrieking and running down the passage! (To this day, I do not know where they went to hide). Noskethi had opened the baboon gate and jumped onto the counter right in front of me. His little eyes had not missed a thing while he was sitting quietly outside the gate. It was Christmas for him, because the fruit bowl on the counter was packed with delicious, juicy fresh fruit! He took a peek into the plastic bag full of vegetable peelings, but was not interested. He stuffed the whole bunch of bananas into his mouth (after peeling them, one by one) and then got stuck into the apples!

Armand and Melanie arrived home just in time to hear the children screaming, and they knew exactly what was going on. I ran out the kitchen door and shouted to Armand to come quickly, Noskethi is in the house! Armand came in and slapped his crocs together, thinking that the noise would frighten Noskethi, but no ways! Armand then disappeared down the passage. I thought he was fetching the broom, but he reappeared with his camera, thinking the flash would frighten Noskethi, but again no ways! He took a couple of snaps and then went to fetch the mop. Noskethi, in the meantime, had polished off almost all the fruit. However, he did not like the look of the 'big stick' in Armand's hands and, before jumping off the counter, took hold of the blue glass dish, held it close against his body and hobbled on two legs and one hand out of the kitchen door and up the driveway. Now, in this glass dish, there were chocolates in paper wrappers! Noskethi was very clever and knew that after Christmas dinner comes Christmas pudding and he was not going to leave his pudding behind!

Noskethi went behind the garage and carefully placed the glass bowl on the lawn. There he sat, taking one chocolate at a time, opening the wrapper and putting the sweet in his mouth. When he had finished, he got up and went for a drink of water, jumped over the fence and disappeared, probably to go and have a well-deserved nap after such a scrumptious Christmas dinner!! He left us ONE chocolate in the bowl.

GREAT excitement was had by all – Ouma, Mom, Dad, Tylan, Keandra AND Noskethi!!

The Frenches are one of the oldest Kommetjie families and the late Dee French had a wealth of stories. Dee was particularly fond of Jane baboon – a dearly loved female baboon from the Slangkop troop. Dee would relate how when she was gardening, Jane would sit quietly next to her, watching with great interest as Dee weeded or planted seedlings. Every now and again Jane would make a grab for a tasty bug or bulb.

The two primates enjoyed many horticultural hours together. Dee was not quite so impressed, however, when one of the large dispersing males came into her home on Christmas Eve. Dee related the following story to me –

I had finished setting the table for Christmas lunch the following day. The Christmas table is a family tradition and the best linen, all the family heirloom crockery and cutlery come out. It looked magnificent, and I was proud of my labour, but tired from all the preparation. As I was heading back into the kitchen I heard a noise in the dining room. I retraced my steps and cautiously peered around the door. There sitting on my beautiful table was a giant male baboon! I didn't know what to do. If I shouted he may have got a fright and jumped off, breaking my mothers' priceless glassware. I was horrified so stood frozen to the spot. To my fascination he merely reached for the silver bowl filled with chocolates, carefully unwrapped a few, ate them and left. The only 'damage' to my Christmas table was that there would be no chocolates after lunch, but there wasn't so much as a dirty footprint, or even one broken item.

He left only some chocolate wrappers and departed as silently as he had arrived.

Dee French

I think that had Dee reacted wildly, the situation may not have turned out nearly as well – it was a tribute to Dee's knowledge of baboon behaviour and her own calm reaction that nothing was broken and that her table arrangement remained intact!

In the stories related in this chapter the common thread is that the people reacted to individual baboons with fascination and amazement, so the damage was minimal. Of course, people are not always so calm, and frequently there is a great deal of mess to clean up and costly damage that most insurance companies won't cover.

Baboons can be hugely destructive, and it is easy for conflict situations to get out of hand quickly. If we are going to live in areas inhabited by baboons we need to learn how to handle ourselves and how to manage our properties.

Only if we understand can we care. Only if we care will we help.
Only if we help shall they be saved....The least I can do is speak out
for those who cannot speak for themselves. **Jane Goodall**

Repetition is the mother of skill... Unknown

Chapter Four

Encouraging bad behaviour

The vast majority of visitors to South Africa, as well as many local residents, have negative encounters with baboons at well-known scenic areas. A common response to these interactions is that the baboons behaved aggressively and stole from them. As a result of these negative experiences all baboons are being cast in a bad light, but is that really fair?

To try to gain some understanding of the situation, it is important to realise that in most cases the baboons have been learning bad behaviour over an extended period of time. We have effectively been training baboons by rewarding them with food. I am sure that none of us intended to embark on baboon training. With the exception of animal behaviourists, most people wouldn't give their own actions a second thought when they do encounter wily baboons; so what am I talking about and how did it all happen?

In baboon society, baboons do not share food. Baboons have to work hard getting their food. In the wild they eat a wide range of bulbs, seeds, flowers and leaves. As they are opportunistic feeders they will also make use of a great variety of other available foods such as insects, even molluscs from the inter-tidal zones, but they don't share. Baboons have a hierarchical system, and so the dominant baboons do just that — they dominate the lower-ranking baboons and steal their food.

A common urban legend is how bigger baboons force the smaller baboons into homes to steal food —

this is not quite true. In reality the smaller ones are every bit as opportunistic as their older relatives, but when they squeeze themselves through small spaces and gain entry into houses for food, they immediately feel a little more vulnerable without the support of the troop, so as quickly as they can they get out of the house, with their hard-won food — only to have the rewards stolen away by the bigger baboons waiting outside!

Baboons have to work too hard digging up bulbs, scratching for seeds and so on to share. The mother baboons do suckle their young — some females will elect to suckle their young for an extended period of nine months to a year — but they still won't willingly share food, even with their offspring. If a baboon becomes sick or injured, I have seen the troop slow down for that individual, but even the sick or injured have to find their own food. Once weaned, each baboon feeds itself.

We humans have a completely different outlook from our baboon cousins. When we see baboons along the side of a road, for example, many of us think that they are there because they must be hungry. Some people want to get great photographs and offer food as an enticement. A few more worrisome individuals like to see baboons fighting over food and deliberately throw food to cause a fight! There are some people who think that they have a special gift or bond with baboons and if baboons take food from them it enhances their ego-driven perception of themselves.

In truth, by feeding baboons we are showing ourselves to be their subordinates. They are not particularly grateful for food given to them, and probably think that we are stupid to give it away so casually.

In the earlier chapters I touched on the fact that baboons weigh up risk versus reward very effect-ively. When we feed them this idea is taken to the next level. Every time a baboon takes food from you, he has been rewarded. If you continually reward any living being for a behavioural pattern then, typically, they repeat the pattern to gain more rewards.

So what we are seeing at Cape Point, Millers Point and many other picnic or scenic routes throughout South Africa is the result of years of training, but we have been rewarding bad behaviour and so the behaviour patterns are now similar to those of an obstreperous three-year-old – demanding, snatching and naughty!

A great many of the stories sent to me reflect just this scenario.

Lee Slabber

Our most recent encounter with baboons was at the Cape Point parking area. We saw no baboons around on arrival but when I started to get out of the car a big one FORCED the door open and as quick as lightening pushed past me and grabbed a bag of fruit. My husband was actually standing outside close by but this did not deter the animal. This was an extremely frightening experience.

When I had recovered we warily walked to the restaurant for breakfast. Whilst we were eating a huge baboon actually entered the seaside door of the restaurant, pinched some muffins from the kitchen and calmly walked out again, fortunately ignoring people eating breakfast.

In the past at Buffels Bay we have had our entire picnic lunch gobbled by a big baboon who stole up behind us and, in spite of being threatened by my husband with his stick, calmly went on eating. We have seen parties of picnickers at Buffels Bay terrified by the approach of a group of baboons and abandoning their fare to the animals.

The worst of our encounters was a few years ago at Chapman's Peak. When we returned to the car from the viewpoint we saw a large baboon nearby, presumably attracted by the presence of a tourist bus. Before my husband could open the car door, the baboon sprang at me, time and time again. I put my arm up to protect my face. We drove away after this shattering experience and when I raised my sleeve of my jacket I found a large gash on my forearm. At False Bay hospital I had an anti-tetanus injection and the wound required ten stitches. After a few weeks the wound looked black and ugly and I had to return to hospital for the area to be scraped out and a skin graft placed on it. I was thus in bandages and in considerable pain for about three months.

We are extremely nervous of baboons as a result of these and other encounters with them. We have had NO pleasant experiences of these animals.

Anne Marshall, Fish Hoek

It is extremely rare that baboons ever do actually bite anyone – from Anne's story I would guess that there had been a great deal of interaction between baboons and tourists during the course of the day and quite possibly there had been negative interactions prior to Anne's arrival. It is difficult to know exactly why the baboon sprang at her, but I can imagine just how frightening and painful the experience must have been.

Brett Cole

Christine Botha and Brian Aldridge also experienced 'baboon muggings' at Cape Point. This is what they had to say —

One bright, sunny summer's day my friend Tony took his family out to Cape Point Nature Reserve for a picnic. Everyone got out of the car and prepared to settle down on the blanket spread out on the grass. As Tony took out the cooler bag, packed with a scrumptious lunch, a big male baboon appeared and promptly tried to grab the bag. Tony held on for dear life and a tug of war ensued — each determined to win. Tony's frightened family hovered near the car and the rest of Mr Baboon's family sat opposite them waiting for the spoils — licking their lips in anticipation. When the baboon became aggressive, baring his huge canines, Tony decided to call it a day. Mr Baboon triumphantly unzipped the bag and ate the delicious food while Tony and family sat watching this spectacle dejectedly from their car. And it must have been quite a sight — watching this lot scoffing their sandwiches, licking out salad containers and even emptying their bottles of cold drink while others got stuck into the pudding and cake!

Christine Botha

And from **Brian Aldridge** –

As a newly-qualified tour guide on my second tour I decided to lay on all the trappings to impress my guests, two charming English ladies who had in their travels had little contact with wildlife especially the precocious baboons of Cape Point. A folding table laden with cold meats, salads, ciabatta and choice of wines was laid out on the white sands of the shore for lunch and the very impressed tourists got stuck into this unexpected feast. The first mouthful brought a flying baboon (yes they can fly — trust me) over a sand dune, crashing onto the pristine white tablecloth. Guests went flying and I into panic mode, not because of fear of superbaboon but that I might lose my hard-earned fees.

In desperation after flapping arms, screaming and shouting 'boggom!' in my most aggressive tone, I grabbed a long piece of dried kelp to beat this lout about the head. By now, his mouth stuffed with a meal for three, he had grabbed the purse of one of the terrified guests with passports and air tickets inside. A coach-load of delighted Chinese tourists pulled up with 35 cameras witnessing my bravery. I chased after the thief waving the kelp which got shorter and shorter as pieces snapped off. Adrenalin pushed me leaping over fynbos, up and down sand dunes in pursuit of the scoundrel who, purse in mouth, kept on looking back at this madness chasing him. Exhausted, he stopped to catch his breath giving me the chance to grab the purse from his mouth. My only defence by now was a 15 cm piece of stinky kelp. To great applause I was redeemed and now take my visitors to a restaurant in Seaforth.

In the stories from both Brian and Christine, it is clear that they were completely unprepared and did not expect baboons to steal their food. They both responded to advances of the baboons differently – but neither got to enjoy their picnic.

Brett Cole

I E Parkin had an equally distressing encounter with baboons at the popular picnic site at Buffels Bay, but this story raises the issue of educating the visitors –

I was in the Cape recently and taken for a picnic lunch of ham rolls and salad to Buffels Bay. We sat on a bench on a high grassy bank, overlooking the sea. We were completely unaware of the presence of two huge female baboons down below, each with a baby clinging to her.

They suddenly appeared from below, bounding straight for us, with teeth bared, and screaming! It was very frightening. We hastily grabbed our belongings and ran up towards our parked car, but one of them attacked our hostess, leaping at her from behind. Fortunately she was wearing a loose-fitting jacket, for it grabbed at the jacket with its teeth, ripping a piece out of it. She fell flat on her face shrieking, and dropped the Tupperware she was carrying, containing the remaining ham roll. The baboon then left her, grabbed the Tupperware and ran away.

The jacket prevented very serious injury. The warning signs are inadequate – "Don't feed the baboons" should be replaced with "Don't picnic with food here, baboons will attack". There could be a fatality.

I E Parkin

47   Beast or Blessing

Although all the stories have illustrated just how scary the baboons can be, there was a sense of humour from Celeste Freedman —

Our god-daughter Melanie came to spend a holiday with us in Cape Town. There isn't much here!

We took her to Cape Point. On the way we stopped to look at the glorious view of sea and mountains. We knew about the baboons and keeping your windows closed!

It was Pesach – Passover time, March or April, so as we don't eat flour at this time, only unleavened food, we took our matzo box with us to have at tea or lunch time. The box was on the back seat next to Melanie.

A huge baboon jumped on the front of the car then moved round the side, opened the back door, jumped in next to Melanie, and took the box of matzo. Melanie didn't utter a sound – we then jumped out of the car.

We always said he must have been a Jewish Baboon!

Celeste Freedman

These encounters are undoubtedly worrying and can be extremely frightening for the individual facing the baboons, especially visitors to the country who have no knowledge of baboons.

Of greater concern to many people are the times when they report: "we didn't even have any food on us – and the baboon still attacked." There is no way to minimise the impact or fear that those situations can create, but if we are to find solutions and change what is happening, we need to really understand the dynamics.

As illustrated by the stories above, the baboons have been learning bad behaviour and have been rewarded for this pattern over many years. During this time the baboons have come to realise that most humans at the scenic spots have some food on them and they know that many vehicles have food inside.

The best analogy to give is that of going through the security check of any airport. In reality, very few of us are actually terrorists, but we all have our bags checked by security systems. The baboons have adopted a similar mindset – but the odds of success are different. Whereas very few of us are terrorists, most of us have some sort of food on us, around us or in our vehicle. So at these specific conflict areas, baboons undertake to 'check' everyone for food – and they are rewarded frequently enough to encourage them to repeat the tactic again and again. Of course, it is not easy for the visitors, or any of us, to accept the baboon strategy easily.

It is unlikely that many of the beautiful scenic picnic spots will be closed off to people and left only to the wildlife – however practical and absolutely ethically correct that solution would be.

We humans are a selfish lot. We have our national parks primarily for our pleasure and do not necessarily consider the best interests of the animals affected by our presence.

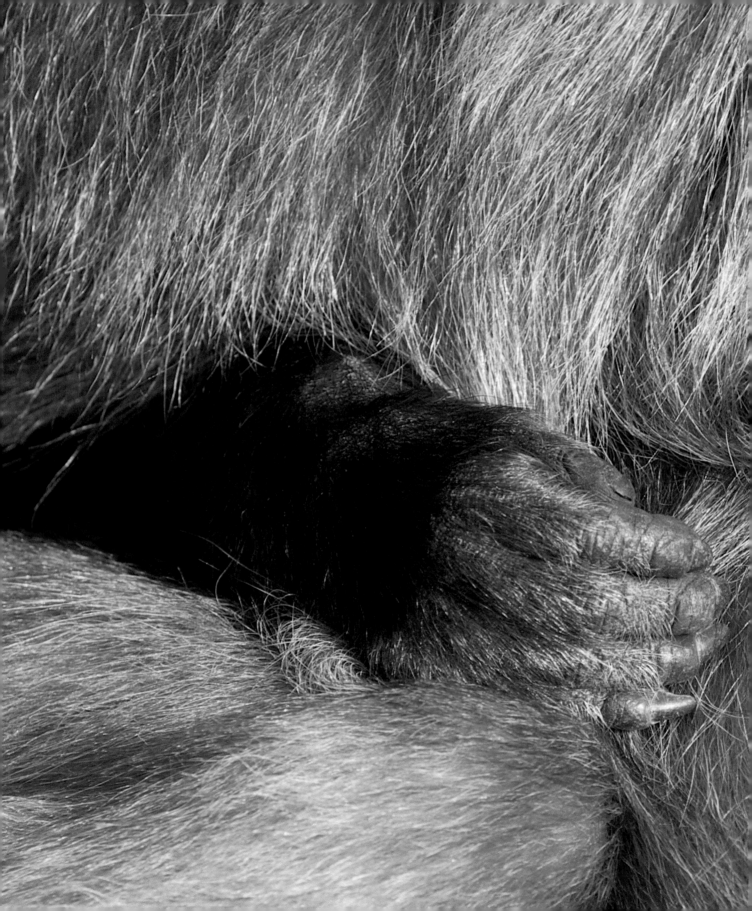

Chapter Five

Management options

For many years it was accepted practice to eliminate so-called problem animals as a management tool. It was only after a small group of Kommetjie residents started the Kommetjie Environmental Awareness Group in 1990 that alternate management options started to be explored. KEAG's first real success came in 1998 when, largely through the efforts of Wally Petersen, baboons were protected from hunting on the Southern Peninsula.

The second success came later in 1998 when the Baboon Management Team decided to pursue another of Wally's ideas – that of baboon monitors.

The idea came about as the conflict situation was escalating and we thought that if we could keep baboons out of the urban areas for as many of the daylight hours as possible, there would be a reduction in clashes between humans and baboons.

The baboon monitors started working in Kommetjie and the men were so good at keeping the baboons out of the village that the project was expanded to include the Da Gama Park and Scarborough troops and later the Tokai troop.

The monitors are extremely successful – the men keep baboons out of the villages where they work for between 60% and 98% of daylight hours. The efficacy of the project does have definite seasonal variations: the excellent natural forage available in spring months means that the monitors are always most effective then, but in the long, hot daylight hours of summer, when the baboons are looking for water and fruiting trees, the efficiency drops.

The fact that the work is so successful is itself noteworthy, as the project battled extreme odds with limited budgets, stop-start funding, lack of manpower and resources. Some residents felt that the monitors were a waste of time, as they didn't understand what the job entailed – or how many problems had to be overcome just to get men in the field.

Luckily a postgraduate student from the University of Cape Town who was undertaking a PhD spent nearly a year gathering data, looking at troop movements and noting the success rate of the monitors. The results of the research were irrevocable – as stated by the University of Cape Town's Baboon Research Unit, monitors are the most effective option for managing baboons.

Despite this, the monitor project has had some negative side effects. The reality is that most residents living in areas affected by baboons simply have no idea what to do to manage their properties and households in such a way that baboons are not attracted into the villages. It is far easier to complain about the monitors rather than to make a small effort to manage your waste effectively, or stop putting food down for guinea fowl and porcupines.

I managed the monitor programme during the difficult years, when there was a pitiful budget, minimal resources and inadequate manpower. I spent hours on the mountain with the monitors, working alongside them, providing transport, fund-raising for uniforms and end-of-year bonuses. I found money for blankets in winter, Christmas braais at year-end and for hospital bills when the men were attacked and robbed, or knocked over by taxis – life in the townships is hard and the salaries we were able to produce on the meagre budget of the project were pathetic. By working so closely with the men, tramping the mountains, getting drenched alongside them, facing the wrath of irate residents and defending them from drunken abusive fools, our bond was forged. It is tough work: gut-wrenching when the baboons are attacked and we rescue their bloodied bodies; depressing when we deal with racist attacks and verbal abuse, but also full of laughs as working with baboons can never keep you bowed for long.

The monitors work long hot hours in summer and spend cold wet hours on the mountains in winter. They have a very physical task as they can spend hours charging up and down steep cliffs after their recalcitrant charges. Yet on the odd occasion when residents see the men watching the baboons, allowing the baboons time to forage or groom, the perception is that the men are not working. This is when residents harass the men for being lazy.

It is a trying job to say the least and compounded by a great deal of ignorance as to what the monitors are actually doing.

Jenni T

Mzukisi Nkewu is one of the original monitors who started working on the project in 1998. Mzukisi was promoted from monitor to supervisor, then field manager. Today he is my 'right-hand man'. I do not know what I would do without Mzukisi. His understanding of baboons and the monitor programme is incredible, as is his loyalty. This is Mzukisi's view on the project —

It is a good plan to monitor the baboons. By monitoring them we protect them from shooting by residents and being bitten by dogs.

If there were no monitors the baboons will be shot and killed then the young generation will only see them on TV and in books.

Have a day off, go and spend that day with them. Watch them when they forage, watch them when they have a rest, grooming each other and watch the juveniles playing, and if they are close to the dam or stream watch them swimming.

But there are some problems we get from residents, we as monitors. When the baboons are in the village the residents shout at us, some don't want us in their properties, they say we are useless. They don't look first why the baboons are in the village before they throw stones at the monitors.

There are things that attract the baboons in the village, namely fruit trees, feeding of guinea fowl, feeding of porcupines — those things attract the baboons.

Mzwakhe Vanga is one of the respected long-standing monitors. Mzwakhe has a deep compassion for the baboons and he hates it when they are injured or killed. He has written this report—

Baboons are clever animals. A baboon is like a person, because they are doing things like us. For example: hide, smell and taste food before they eat. They care for the babies, also they feed the babies on their breasts. Also they give hugs to each other. They keep the babies on their back like a person.

As I understand, baboons are not dangerous animals to people. Because they just only look for food. Don't feed the baboons. If you feed them you are in trouble. Because if you feed them for one day, they keep on coming to look for food in your house. At the end they get inside the houses and look for food. The baboons are not robbing, they are just looking for some food. All these things are because of the residents, they feed them. It is not allowed to feed the baboons. The important thing is the residents are building the houses and staying in the baboons' places. At the end of the day, the residents are complaining because of the baboons. They forget they build houses in the baboons' places. There's nothing wrong about baboons. It is only that people abuse baboons. They forget a baboon is a very clever animal. Also if you want to learn about the animals learn about the baboons. The baboons know about the dustbin days. They sleep close to the villages on those days because they know in the morning it is a dustbin day. Between baboons and monitors it is like a competition because the baboons wake up very early on the dustbin day. They know the monitors will come.

Do not carry food in front of the baboons. They are not attacking people, they are taking food to eat.

Jenni Trethowan

Trevor de Kock

Enoch Sityi has been a baboon monitor for almost seven years now and he had this to say about his job —

The best job you can ever have is the one you would love. The job I'm doing is very interesting to me. You get contact with nature. I have learnt a lot from my job: the behaviour of the animals and the way they interact with each other.

You will find that baboons protect their young ones, and they live in packs. Their togetherness taught me a lot, such as how we could also practise some of the things they do in our own families. They can some-times be a handful but it comes with the job. You have to love them because they have been wonder-fully created by God.

It makes me sad that some people kill these animals. That's why we protect them so that they may not be extinct. Our grandchildren and their children may also see them and not hear or see them in history books. That's what keeps me going, and this love I have for nature.

Mawethu Ndyawe is one of the newer monitors, having joined the project in 2008. He has some ideas that the residents should know about —

I like this job to be a monitor because it makes me learn about a lot of things such as nature, animals and how they live. Most of all I like to work with baboons because most of the things they do are the same that people do.

Talking about a monitor and a resident, some of the residents don't understand to be a monitor. It prevents troops from entering the residential areas. Some of them they understand what we are doing.

Sometimes the residents don't want the monitors entering the properties so they make our job so hard, because our job is to keep the baboons out of the residential areas, and to maintain the baboon troop within their natural environment.

My suggestion is to let the monitors into your properties, it will help you and us. I like my job as a monitor.

Vuyani has been working with the project for almost five years and is one of the very fit and athletic men employed to keep baboons out of the villages. Here are his thoughts —

I am Vuyani Fete. I grew up in a small town called Alice in Eastern Cape. In our house we have many cows and as a small boy it was my duty to look after the cows. Even after school, I was supposed to go and look if the cows are in a safe environment. I left school in Standard 8 because of personal reasons. I left the Eastern Cape and travelled to Cape Town to look for a job. I found a job to look after baboons. I found this job in 2004.

I have learnt so many things as a baboon monitor because when you are a monitor you must have strength. To be a monitor is not easy: you walk up and down the whole day. The baboons are just like us as human beings. They do exactly what humans do, even the way they are treating their families.

So as monitor I am 100% sure that we are helping many people because if we are not there as monitors there is much damage.

My friend it needs perseverance, strength and spirit to overcome until you finish the day.

We must respect each other.

John Yeld

Despite the problems that usually go with employing people, on the whole, I built a great team, and relished my time working with the monitors. The laughs outweighed the heartache time and again. I have a wealth of memories associated with the monitors, many funny, some sad, some reflecting the anger, but the following story illustrates my respect and bond with the monitors –

It was the long days of summer, hot and dry, and by the end of each day you knew you had done a day and a half of work. I was visiting the team on Slangkop Mountain behind Kommetjie. We had been battling to get the troop out of the village as the attractions of the waste were just irresistible but, with a lot of hard effort, that afternoon the baboons were back on the mountain.

The baboons were relaxed, foraging at the end of the afternoon before heading off to their sleep site. It is always a magnificent sight to see the baboons moving through the fynbos where they should be, not in the villages or rummaging through dustbins.

When I arrived I was pleased to note that the monitors had planned well and were ranged on the rocks at various points so the baboons would see them and know there would be a deterrent if they attempted to get back to Kommetjie.

I greeted the men and then sat on a rock watching the baboons and letting the men make the decisions, as I wanted to check on the end-of-day procedures. After a while the baboons started heading to their sleep site on the cliffs. Taking their cue from the baboons, the men started to follow and as one, the men and baboons ambled away – the baboons grabbing the occasional leaf or seed head to eat as they went.

It was indescribably beautiful with the golden glow of late afternoon, the incredible scenery and the troop moving together.

Suddenly one of the monitors started to sing – his rich voice rising with joy into the afternoon sky. One by one the others joined in – harmonising effortlessly. And so, singing with gusto, the monitors walked slowly behind the baboons as they moved to their sleep site – and it was one of the most privileged moments of my life.

Although the baboon monitors are hugely effective at what they do, for baboon management to be truly successful, all residents who live in areas affected by baboons need to play an active role in making their properties unattractive to baboons.

I received a divergent range of stories from residents, but the following two stories stood out – mainly for their humour!

Nicholas Trethowan

Dear Sir/Madam

My name is Hardy Grun. Living in Barrydale on my farm. Last year a group of approximately 12 baboons came several times around lunchtime and raided the nests of my geese, eating all the eggs. I put up a scarecrow, hung up plastic snakes for several hundred rand. Totally useless.

So I went on lookout to chase them.

One day I see them approaching. I went outside. When they discovered me, the leader started shouting at me.

So I shouted back at him in the same manner. He shouted, I shouted back. It went on for more than an hour. After a while he and his group started receding, always for several metres and then shouting again. I will not translate for you in English what I shouted, but it worked. Since that time they never came back.

The question is – do I speak baboon?

Regards
Hardy Grun

Dave Rattle of Capri Village tried a completely different approach —

Whenever we talk about baboons with Annie's brother John he always brings up the following incident with a chuckle – for him, apparently, it was high humour!!

A few years ago we were together at Partridge Point, along the False Bay coastline, the Smitswinkel side of Castle Rock. We were inspecting a property there. When we got back to the bakkie there was a small troop of baboons sitting beside it playing and grooming and there was also a very large male – sitting right on top of the canopy. To access the vehicle we obviously had to do something.

I don't remember why, but I landed up at the back end of the vehicle whilst the others were at the front. They started making 'shoo, shoo, baboon' noises as they walked slowly forward with the intention of gently moving the troop away, but meanwhile there I was, right in the path of their retreat! The smaller females and the babies soon moved and, taking no notice of me, drifted on past, but the big male didn't budge from the roof until the very last minute.

Then suddenly, galvanised into action, he vaulted down and headed straight at me, very fast indeed! Aggression! Oh my lord! This was it!

With no chance of moving out of the way, this was my time – quite certainly the way I would go! Mauled to death by a giant 'silverback'! My life flashed before my eyes, but also some race memory that told me – be submissive! Avert your eyes! Turn your back! Show him your bum!

That suited me fine – it was as much an automatic attempt at major flinching from the anticipated impact as trying to be clever and 'act baboon', and I turned around fast and bent down like a naughty schoolboy with my backside presented to the headmaster.

And then, suddenly, he was past me but, as he went, he delivered a hefty whack on my raised posterior – a contemptuous thwackka-whakka-whack that said to me in no uncertain terms: "Now bugger off and stop annoying me - AND DON'T GET IN MY WAY AGAIN!!" And let me tell you, I never have!!

Brett Cole

Neither Harvey or Dave's management styles seemed to have worked for them.

In the past eleven years, the Baboon Monitoring Project has lurched from funding crisis to funding crisis – but has kept going and achieved success where many other projects would have folded.

Regrettably the downside of this successful project has been that residents of areas where the monitors do operate have generally become lackadaisical in their individual efforts to manage their properties effectively. It is too easy to point your finger and blame the monitors for not working properly, when in reality aspects such as the lack of waste management, fruiting trees and even putting grains down for guinea fowl and other birds, all attract baboons into the villages.

For baboon management to be truly effective all residents and role players have to be in agreement and work towards the same goals. Baboons have been a contentious topic for hundreds of years, and today we are no closer to agreement than we were years ago. The pity is that there is no real rocket science involved, just common sense and a bit of effort – and agreement from your neighbours! Of course, therein lies the problem – how will we ever be in agreement with our neighbours?

Some of us follow the rules slavishly, others will always have a better plan. There are those who believe in the abundance theory – that there is plenty for everyone and we must all learn to share – whilst others believe that pain aversion will have the best results.

Despite the divergent opinions, there is one area that more than 70% of residents do agree on – that is they do not want to see the baboons exterminated ever again.

And there is unanimous agreement that they don't want baboons raiding their homes or their villages. Perhaps, using these two agreements as the building blocks, we can start to find more and more common ground so that we all work together and not rely too heavily on any single aspect of baboon management.

ethowan

Gina du Plessis

Why I study baboons

by Dr Timothy K. Newman

In the summer of 1995 I spent three months in the Awash National Park in central Ethiopia, tracking and observing two species of baboon ('Desert' vs 'Savanna') living in a geographically and ecologically defined hybrid zone. I had already studied their mitochondrial DNA, and now I was able to witness a natural experiment in speciation, revealed by the physical evidence of gene flow between the source populations.

I recall my time in the field vividly, but one singular experience stands out. We were habituating a large troop in the middle of the hybrid zone, getting them accustomed to our presence by distributing dried corn. As they fed we sat quietly, observing their interactions. Most of the members of this troop were true hybrids, showing intermediate morphology in skin and coat color. In baboons, physical and behavioral differences between species are most pronounced in adult males, and the differences between the Desert and Savanna populations I studied were particularly stark.

As I watched the members of the troop going about their activities I was struck by the degree to which males behaved strongly in accordance with their phenotype. That is, Savanna-like hybrids were prone to chasing each other and fighting, as do typical Savanna baboons, while Desert-like hybrids were more likely to corral their females in typical Desert baboon fashion. The intermediate hybrid males, however, displayed stereotypical behaviors that were just as intermediate as their external characteristics. Anthropomorphasising a bit, it was as if the hybrid males were torn between wanting to get into the chase versus guarding their mates. Each male's response to a specific stimulus (e.g contest over food or the perception of being challenged) varied, and was largely determined by the heritable gene variants that characterize and distinguish Desert from Savanna baboons.

We had a window on the evolutionary process, and the experience had a profound and lasting impact on my research interests.

Br

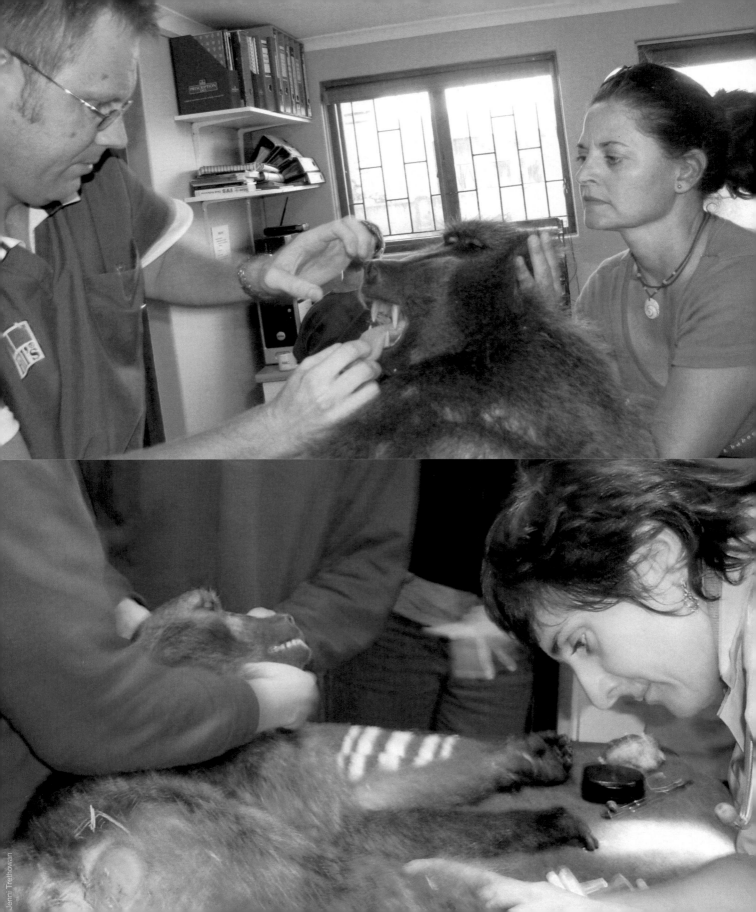

Chapter Six

Healing the hurts

One of the grim realities of the conflict between people and baboons is the injuries inflicted on the baboons by intolerant people. It is difficult to understand why people would elect to hurt the baboons in the ways that they do. Having had my own home trashed on more than one occasion, gutters pulled down, food eaten, etc, I fully understand that baboons do cause a great deal of damage. I also know only too well how extremely irritating it is to have to clean up after the baboons – especially when you have already had a long, hard day at work. And those of us who have cleaned up after baboons know just what a mess they can make!

What I struggle to understand though, is this concept that hurting the baboons will solve the problem. The conflicts between us and baboons have been going on for hundreds of years now, and to date hurting the animals has not solved anything at all.

In reality, the only thing that happens when people take their tempers out on the baboons is that baboons get hurt. Some get hurt very badly, and some die – but the problem doesn't go away.

Over the years I have rescued many, many baboons. The Baboon Matters team has developed our strategy and equipment to deal specifically with the intelligence of baboons. Our early mistakes in the field have helped us refine our approach and the result is that we are generally able to get the injured baboon very quickly, and with a minimum of stress to the animal.

As baboons are incredibly resilient and recover from wounds and injuries that would keep us in hospital for months, we only go out to rescue a baboon if the situation is really serious. So on the occasions when we do have to rescue an individual, it is in extreme circumstances and we are never complacent about the suffering. It has been amazing over the years to see how the baboons trust us, and how they inevitably seek eye contact.

No-one who looks into the eyes of an injured baboon can fail to be moved or humbled.

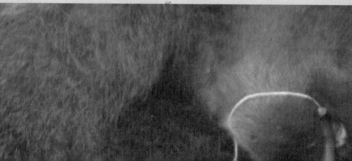

One of the stories sent to me regarding helping injured baboons came from Pippa and Jurie Moolman, who run the beautiful game lodge Djuma. Pippa describes a particularly busy day at the lodge –

Jurie set off for the bush to bring the hyena back home to prepare it for his skeleton collection. Then another radio call came through to Jurie. This time the alert was for a baboon that had been sending distress calls from an old, abandoned reservoir near Dixie village. Because Jurie was busy with the hyena he asked Steve Baillie and Jimmy Hurlimann, both guides at Djuma, to go out to the reservoir and find out what was going on. It turned out that there was not one, but about twenty young baboons stuck inside the reservoir. We reckoned that the larger baboons, and the babies that could hang onto their mothers, had managed to get out, but the teenagers were too small to make the climb to freedom. Jimmy and Steve lowered a branch into the reservoir and several of the stronger baboons struggled to safety, leaving five very weak individuals among others already dead, lying in the putrid muck at the bottom of the reservoir. The guys hauled the five survivors out, wrapped them in the blankets from the game-drive vehicle, and brought them back to our house. In the meantime we had phoned our mate, Wally Petersen, in the Cape for advice. Wally was the right guy to call as he had been involved for years with baboon research on the Cape Peninsula and, in fact, had also once rescued some baboons from a similar predicament. The first thing we had to do was to wash and warm the baboons to revive them from hypothermic shock. From the appalling state of their dehydrated and thin bodies we reckoned that the baboons must have been trapped for a week or more. One by one they were bathed in the children's tub, and then wrapped up in towels and blankets. As Wally pointed out, we were fortunate they were so weak, as they were easy to handle. If they had been stronger they could have put up a hell of a fight, when their long canines would have been dangerous. The bathroom now smelt like a sewer, with most surfaces spattered in green goo. The next thing we did was to clear our garden guest-room of furniture and fire up a gas heater. The baboons took turns at warming up slowly in the tattooed arms of Steve and Jimmy, with Jurie and Campbell assisting. They were too weak to eat and, anyway, in the state they were in, solid food would have been too much for their systems to handle. Wally told us to mix isotonic fluids and feed them via babies' bottles, which we did. It was quite endearing to see these bush guys cradling the baboons in their arms and coaxing them to drink. Within a few hours the baboons were stabilized enough to start moving around and drink for themselves from bowls filled with the hydrating fluids. The following morning they were given grated apple.

The next task was to get them to leave of their own accord, which was not as easy as expected because they had no inclination to venture through the open door. We decided to play baboon vocalisations over a tape recorder, which worked, in that the local Gowrie troop started responding with their own calls. This was enough to entice our little ones into the bush. The weakest one, which Steve called Leroy, was not keen to leave the yard and hung around for a few days, living off the titbits we left for him and the gum exuded from the acacia trees in our garden. He did eventually leave and join up with the rest of the troop. We suspect that the Gowrie troop may share a common boundary with the Dixie troop, so there was a good chance of the five survivors getting back to their families of origin. To ensure there would be no repeats of that episode we put a ladder in the reservoir.

Out at Djuma, Pippa and Jurie are able to deal with most problems that come their way themselves, and calling a vet in is not common practice at all. Here in Cape Town, we rely heavily on our veterinarians for their assistance. Over the years a few vets have built up a great deal of expertise in dealing with baboons – as you can imagine baboons are not your average veterinary patient.

Jenni T

When she was at Fourways Veterinary Clinic, Dr Gina du Plessis gained more than her fair share of practice on baboons – and no matter how busy Fourways is, when I phone to say we are on the way with an injured baboon, they know that our cases are all emergencies and do everything they can to assist. Gina had some very grim cases to deal with, not all of them had pleasant outcomes, but the story of Thami was one of the happier stories –

What I am about to write is a simple story, a sad story, the truth about the life of a young baboon living in the mountains of the Cape Peninsula. It is a story that has affected me profoundly, partly because I became intrinsically involved in decisions that affected the course of her life and partly that I still rally at so many things in this world that are just so unfair, and cause so much suffering to the innocent. This is a story though that has not reached its conclusion and because of this fact, it is a story that still has hope.

It was 2005. My day at the clinic was following very much its normal hectic flow.

Suddenly the call came: INJURED BABOON – ON WAY TO CLINIC. What this meant was that at any time in the next hour or so, a darted baboon would come through the front door, with some form of injury – gunshot wounds, stab wounds, poisoning, motor vehicle accident. Mostly when these baboons come in they require immediate assistance either due to the nature of the injury or because they have been darted and can only be worked on while sleeping/under anaesthetic. These are wild animals that are obviously stressed and in pain. We're talking fluids (drips), painkillers, antibiotics, gastric lavage, X-rays, surgery or any combination of the aforementioned depending on the case. If surgery is required, it is normally needed straight away.

Virtually everything at the clinic comes to a standstill, at least for one of the veterinarians. WHAT WERE WE GOING TO BE FACED WITH THIS TIME? She was a three-year-old little girl with multiple gunshot wounds, that we had not met before, a very unlucky little individual that we would come to know as Thami – a derivative of a Xhosa word meaning 'Lucky', so-named by the monitors, the baboon guardian angels, for surviving. She was darted and dazed, bloodied and in shock. Drips, painkillers, anaesthetics and X-rays followed, and we discovered the worst. The bullet had struck her in the femur of her right leg and had completely shattered the bone. I attempted surgery but realized that the leg was fractured beyond repair, it could not be pinned or plated. What to do now? Two options remained, amputate her leg or euthanase her right there on the theatre table. A brief but crucial meeting followed in the operating theatre. No previous knowledge or documentation of amputating the limb of a baboon existed. To my best knowledge it had not been done before. What did we do? All we could do was weigh up the pros and cons – she was young; it was a back leg and foot, not a front limb; she could be returned to the troop after recovery and monitored. If she could not cope, she could always be darted and removed from the troop. Let's face it, if it were you or me, or any living being, we would like to be given the benefit of the doubt. If we didn't give it to her, she would have everything to lose – HER LIFE.

Well, I amputated that limb and Thami woke up, not feeling quite so lucky. She was young and resilient and recovered well and quickly, amazingly so. But then again animals are great in that they get on with life, they don't seem to suffer the psychological ordeal us humans do with the physical loss of a body part. They seem to get over it and move on. I will however never forget her sitting in the corner of the clinic's recovery cage, examining her left hind leg and foot, seemingly counting her toes, moving over to the right limb…nothing there. It seemed that in her head she was trying to work this one out, as she fingered the nylon sutures on the swollen stump. They were indeed a sad substitute for toes.

It took a few days for her to get her balance right, and within a week to 10 days she was doing well enough for us to consider her release. In fact, she was craving release and she made it very obvious.

The next phase was upon us, Jenni had to organize her release. But so many questions remained. What was the troop's reaction going to be towards this crippled member? Only time would tell.

On the morning of her release we were all a bit nervous, not knowing what to expect. The monitors started out early to find the troop – they were at Glencairn's Navy sports fields. We would meet them there. Thami was not sedated and on the way over to Blackhill, it became evident just how excited she was becoming, smelling and sensing that we were approaching her home ground.

She was released several hundred metres from the troop, by now bumping and thumping inside the box to get out. She was beside herself with excitement and anticipation.

What I saw next I will not forget as long as I live. Once the cage door was opened, the little girl shot out and sprinted to her family as fast, agile and athletic as any four-limbed creature would be. For a brief moment I thought we had released the wrong baboon! I would never have guessed she was an amputee! She covered those dividing metres with unbelievable speed. The troop started howling and screaming, with what must have been initial surprise, shock, fright, who knows. Very soon it turned into screams and hollers of wild joy and greetings. What a raucous welcoming. We had been worried that the troop may turn on her because she must have smelled of humans, clinic and medicine. Because she was now different – very different and possibly even a burden – most wild animals would have attacked her. But not these baboons! They touched her, smelled her, welcomed her back into the troop and it took no more than five minutes for the excitement to die down. "Hi kiddo – welcome back, good to see you, okay, let's get on with the day and get out of here." So within minutes all the baboons settled down and eventually moved off slowly, foraging as they went. Jenni pointed out to me that Thami was closely accompanied by her mother as she moved up the mountainside.

At that moment I felt as if my heart was going to burst out of my chest. I loved and respected these baboons even more than before. I knew then that we had made the right decision to give Thami this chance to make a life out there on three limbs.

Time passed and whenever there was news of Thami it was good. She was coping, it seemed, better than we all could have imagined. So well in fact that about a year later Jenni's excited voice on the phone was informing me that Thami was now a young mother to a beautiful little boy. They named him Trevor. Who was the dad? Well, who better than dear old George, the head of the troop. And best of all, I was invited to go and have a look for myself. It was early days, there was considerable concern that the baby may not survive given that Thami was a first-time mom. Many of these babies do not survive, and the fact that she was an amputee made matters so much more difficult for her. Could she make the grade? I waited just a few weeks and booked a walk on my weekend off. I couldn't wait! Loaded with cameras and eager anticipation, I saw her sitting on a rock, with her right leg missing. I didn't notice at first, but glued to her chest was a small pink-faced and pink-eared imp, wearing a very content but mischievous expression. I was so pleased. Trevor was about five

to six weeks old and Thami was doing a splendid job. She seemed to manage well in carrying him. He clung to her for dear life. Always gnawing away in the back of my mind were my concerns: he is going to grow and get heavier and more demanding. How will she cope? Oh go away doubt and reason – SHE IS DOING GREAT AND SO IS HE!

Cameron Mc Donald

I had such fun filming and videoing. It was a perfect sunny Saturday morning in Cape Town and some of my best scenes were filming George and Thami with little Trevor playing between them. Thami fussed with the youngster and George tolerated it with immense paternal patience. We all thought we could hear George say: "Now Thami dear, stop spoiling the boy, you'll turn him into a brat if you're not careful," and we laughed. Oh God, it was a day for laughter, one filled with joyful, picture-perfect scenes, a sad story with a near-miraculous ending.

But that was not to last for long. Trevor had not quite reached his sixth month on this planet, when he was tragically killed on the Kommetjie road when attempting to cross the road alongside his mother. It broke my heart.

This time Thami's loss was that much more painful, the loss of a first-born child, conceived and raised against all odds. Three-limbed Thami was not capable of getting her child out of the road in time.

This is the story of Thami. Thami the Brave, Thami the Three-Limbed. For her, I still believe being alive and having suffered loss is better than not having had a chance at life at all. Thami is young and still has a lot of living to do. Her story is not finished yet. My wish for her is to live to a ripe old age without any further loss or pain at the hands of man. A dream, probably wishful thinking on my part.

It would certainly go a long way to restore my faith in mankind and our future. Help me to forgive mankind for what I have seen them do to one another and animals in particular, especially to baboons. BABOONS MATTER.

As for little Trevor, what can I say? Nothing can change his destiny now, his story has been written. No surgery or drips or amputations can give him a chance, or even half a chance like his mother had. At least he cannot suffer anymore at the hands of man and will not have to be around to see which way the dice falls. Will enough people care to give his family and other baboons back the land that rightfully belongs to them? Maybe leave enough land for them just to be able to survive? I hope that Trevor has joined the spirit of his ancestors, who, not so long ago, still had the God-given right to roam this beautiful peninsula without human interference. Little Trevor — you were a symbol of hope — and then we lost you too — I am so sorry.

Goodbye sweet Trevor,
You have not gone forever,
But have a place in our hearts.
We all had a happy time
And your life was sublime.
Trevor, your mom had only three paws,
But her love had no flaws.
You were one of God's doves,
No wonder everyone fell in love
With your sweet, innocent face —
You were one of a beautiful race.
You might have been quite small
But your sweet care over-ruled us all.
Goodbye young Trevor
We will remember you forever.

Nicholas Trethowan, aged 11

The man who kills animals today is the man who kills people who get in his way tomorrow...**Dian Fossey**

Cape Argus

Not all veterinary assistance is for surgery or medical intervention. If we are trying to capture a dispersing male baboon, then vets are required to come along with the team and dart the baboon if we have been unable to capture him in a trap cage. As baboons are so incredibly smart, it is seldom that you capture them in a cage twice, so inevitably the dispersing males are captured the first time, but then have to be darted on their second foray into suburbia.

Darting a baboon in busy, densely built-up areas can be extremely time-consuming and frustrating! You no sooner get the baboon into a 'dartable' position, than a member of the public decides he/she knows best how to catch a baboon and their efforts upset hours of preparation and the baboon gets chased off. There are so many variable factors that come into play that darting one male baboon can take days in the field, kilometres of running up and down streets – and vast amounts of patience.

Jenni Tre

There are not many domestic vets who have either the equipment or experience to dart baboons. In Cape Town we have one such vet – Dr Hamish Currie. Hamish has been called out to help dart in all conditions – and invariably it is on a public holiday or a weekend that he and my team find ourselves running along a railway line, or clambering over roofs of dilapidated buildings in pursuit of a determined male baboon. Here is one of Hamish's shorter encounters –

The tale of a travelling man
by Dr Hamish Currie

One of our more famous baboons on the Peninsula is a certain John Wayne who decided on New Year's Day 2008 the time was right to get onto a ship in Cape Town harbour. Was his intent an exotic trip to some palm-fringed island? Or was there another motive? At a time when our country has a few problems, many intellectuals jump on ships and leave the country for greener pastures.

Maybe there is a message here. Our baboons are brighter than we think!

I decided this was now a real emergency and collected my kit together to dart him and get him off the ship. However Jenni Trethowan cleverly trapped him and released him back on the mountain where he belonged. John however had different ideas and was soon back in the urban space doing his thing.

It was decided we had to catch him and release him in Cape Point Nature Reserve. There are no palm trees there but we all thought the presence of nubile baboon maidens at the reserve might be enough to keep him there.

Kira Joshua and other members of the SPCA, myself and the South African police made up the team. John was in Retreat being followed by hundreds of locals baying for his blood.

When I arrived with dart-gun in hand they thought the idea was that we were going to shoot him. "Maak hom dood. Skiet hom! Skiet hom!" they shouted. Sirens blaring, people shouting: poor John was in the wrong place. His life was at risk.

By some miracle I got a dart into him on the roof of the Zwaanswyk school. As the drug took effect, he started sliding down on the roof of the second floor. It was a long way to drop.

Was this to be his undignified end? Luckily his foot wedged against the gutter and he stopped sliding. Phew! We were sweating. A ladder was found and Kira was up there in a flash. John was waking up. Now I am not known for my mountaineering skills but I gingerly made my way up to help Kira. Ropes were procured and we lowered him down where he was safely put in a cage. Gotcha!

We have had a case of TB in a peninsula baboon so it is our responsibility to TB-test all baboons who are being moved around. It would be irresponsible to spread disease. We injected tuberculin into his eyelid and put him in a cage for 72 hours to check for a reaction. Luckily John was negative.

John is one of the gentlest baboons I have worked with. When we pole-syringed him, his reaction was a pathetic grunt. His amber eyes appeared to have no malice even though we had him in prison.

John now has a bright yellow tag in his ear. If you see him have some compassion for this beautiful creature as my instinct tells me he is a good man, just sometimes a little wayward. After all, nobody is perfect.

Jenni

John Wayne gained a certain notoriety after his exploits on the ship – he was featured on the front pages of newspapers across the USA and in some countries in Europe. Although he was undoubtedly a celebrity baboon, the story of John Wayne did not have a happy ending. Even though he settled well in the Plateau Road troop of baboons, he mysteriously vanished one day and was never seen again. The victim of yet another shooting? We will never know for sure but hope that John Wayne did not suffer – he was a wonderful character and deserved better.

When you work with sick or injured animals, there is something about the patient that touches the healer and one of the things that I have noticed is that the people assisting with injured baboons often receive some healing themselves.

Noskethi is a remarkable male baboon who has touched the lives of many Welcome Glen residents, but none more so than Peggy and her husband Paul. Peggy is one of those rare people who see good in everything and always seems to be nursing a sick bird or giving love and attention to a stray cat.

I believe that Noskethi turned to Peggy for support after he had been severely wounded. He seemed to know instinctively that he would have a safe haven with Peggy and Paul and he spent weeks at Peggy's house living alongside his two human carers. It was one of the most remarkable and endearing things I have ever seen. Peggy and Paul would sit outside with their coffee in the morning and Noskethi would forage on the grass around the table – the peace and tranquillity of the scene an oasis from the chaos of typical baboon-Welcome Glen interactions. Here is Peggy Rhynes's story –

For three years I used to watch the baboons of George's troop visiting our garden at the campsite at Glencairn. I loved watching the way they interacted as a family, kids even getting a hiding if they stepped over the line, sometimes playing in our swimming pool, but for hours one lone baboon got my attention. He used to come and just sit, watching my three wild cats living under a bush, never harming them – just lying in the sun.

One day I heard a strange noise by my back door and found Noskethi sitting looking at me, covered in blood. His eyes seemed to be pleading, please help me, I trust you.

I contacted Jenni Trethowan and told her, and while waiting for her to arrive I spoke soothingly to him. That day our bond started.

After his treatment at the vet, he made his way back to my place where he stayed on and off for about three months.

Those were times I will never forget. I had an old couch on my stoep he used as a bed, lying on it just as a human would. He would watch me and my husband have tea in the morning at our stoep table

and next thing he was sitting just like us, eating some nuts in his dish. Whenever my husband left his hammer on the table he would place his hand over it and wait till he fetched it.

He used to walk with him to work and then lie on the field under the trees watching Paul at work. At night he would climb in a tree outside our bedroom window, although it caused him a lot of pain because of his injuries.

When I did my housework, he used to sit and watch me by my security gate. He never tried to damage anything on my property. He was always a real gentleman. He used to jump over my garden gate till I showed him it could open, then he used to push it open. Whenever I looked into his beautiful brown eyes, I felt such a love for him and will forever cherish the love, trust and friendship he offered me.

I respect baboons and on their behalf I would like to ask people to do their share to prevent them also becoming extinct.

Can you imagine a world without animals? We are encroaching on their territory, the mountains, they were there first!

Jenni T

Noskethi - A lasting impression
by Rosemary Ashleigh, Welcome Glen

Like many residents living in Welcome Glen, I've had several close-up encounters with the troop when they raid our village, and as a result had become pretty wary of them! Then one day in the early spring of 2005 I bumped into Jenni on the outskirts of my village. She was searching for an injured baboon so she invited me to join her. At a stream in the valley, I suddenly found myself surrounded by a troop of baboons. My horror and nervousness was soon put to rest with Jenni's coaxing, and then we were off up the hill to come to rest finally alongside a huge injured male baboon called Noskethi. I was extremely nervous, but stayed — mesmerized and fascinated. The next day Jenni decided he needed to be darted as his condition had worsened and he required medical attention. She asked me to watch him while she went off to make the necessary arrangements for his capture.

So, there I was, alone with one of our blue planet's most wonderful creatures. I have lived in many bushveld areas and have had encounters with many different types of wild animals. But never in a million years did I expect such a life-changing experience, here on the southern peninsula of the Western Cape. For the next four hours we sat together in tall kikuyu grass, sheltering from the cold north-westerly wind. I did all the talking and crying, while he did all the moaning and groaning. That's how we got to know each other and that's how I fell in love with baboons — especially with Noskethi. I cried buckets — happy and sad tears, the way only a girl can! My sadness was for the unnecessary pain and cruelty inflicted on baboons; my happiness was for the pure joy of the experience. Each time he opened his eyes to look at me, I couldn't believe the beauty reflected – he seemed to hold a mixture of the ancient universe and the new world in his eyes. We think we see a lot in our pets' eyes, but you ain't seen nothing yet till you've looked into the amber eyes of a baboon! There's so much trust, gentleness and wisdom, it's breathtaking. Weeks later, after a full recovery and having spent much of his time on his own, he rejoined his troop – only to get caught in a vicious fight with one of the males of the troop. I went off on my own to see how Noskethi was doing. I had brought my digital camera so I could photograph his wounds and email them to Jenni for her to assess the extent of his wounds. Blood was pouring from a wound on his chest, which I could easily photograph, but the wound at the back of his neck was concealed by thick fur.

I had by now learnt a lot more about baboons and of their close genetic relationship to humans; and that an adult apparently has the mentality of a small human child – so, this time, I decided to try to 'communicate' with him.

I sat down behind him to take a photograph. Feeling incredibly daft and hoping no-one was around to hear me, I asked him to move his head so I could photograph the wound. I must have rephrased my sentence about three times, communicating as one would with a two or three-year-old child, using the simplest language possible, when suddenly and most unexpectedly his hand reached up behind his head and he brushed his fur aside, maintaining the posi-

tion in order for me to see the wound clearly. I was so stunned and shocked that I froze. Then his hand started moving away; I quickly snapped with hands shaking with excitement, so it ended up being a bit blurred! Unfortunately, the camera click startled Noskethi – he suddenly turned around baring his teeth at me – a frightening sight! But I had got to know him, and knew he was a gentleman, so in a very quiet voice I said "It's okay, Noskethi, it's fine. I'm not trying to harm you," and slowly moved the camera away. My nerves were finished! I thought my heart would explode, but he understood that too, and just looked at me. His beautiful amber eyes captivated mine once more.

When I told him how sorry I was he couldn't join the troop that night, he got up, looked over his shoulder towards their sleep site, gave the most heart-breaking drawn-out cry and moved off in the direction of his safe haven. My heart broke for him – he was making it perfectly clear how sad and lonely he was.

Noskethi returned to his troop time and time again – eventually maintaining his position as a fully mature male in the troop and fathering babies of his own. I've had the privilege of many many wonderful and very special encounters with baboons since; and I've got to know and love many others, but none will ever fill that very special place Noskethi has in my heart. He taught me how to 'be' with his kind – how to communicate and understand in return; and for that I'm eternally grateful. Jenni and Noskethi – thank you for introducing me to the wonderful world of baboons.

Babysitting Blues

by Heather Holthysen, Welcome Glen

I received a call from Jenni Trethowan of Baboon Matters asking if I would like to babysit a little one-week-old baby baboon the next day. I think Jen knew the answer long before she phoned me and immediately received an emphatic and ecstatic YES! Then I felt guilty as I thought: how on earth could I feel so excited when there must surely be a traumatic reason why the baboon needed looking after in the first place. Living in Welcome Glen, where baboons are maligned at best and abused, maimed or killed at worst by some of the arrogant and intolerant residents of this beautiful village, I knew that yet another awful event must have taken place.

I'm afraid I am selfish enough to admit that nevertheless, I was so excited, I could hardly sleep, with thoughts leaping through my head all night, like, what should a human surrogate baboon mom wear, smell like and do, to make a teeny and surely traumatised baby baboon feel better? Anyway, by morning common sense prevailed and I went dressed in normal (but cosy!) clothes and smelling like a normal human being, just without perfume!

On the way, I remembered the orphan baby I had seen at The Manger sanctuary in Barrydale a few weeks ago, run by Nola and Peter Frazer. In order to survive and at least get some sleep, Nola had put Guinevere into nappies at night. So I stopped off for the smallest disposable nappies I could find – newborn! Thus armed I arrived at Jenni's house,

ready for action and almost ecstatic at the thought I was about to hold a weeny baby in my arms for the first time in 25 years.

Well, my life tilted when I saw that baby. In an instant it was LOVE. When I clutched her to me as a baboon mom would have, there was no more than a little squawk from her as she snuggled in under my armpit. Oh my, what a moment. A surge of love as strong as when I held my own newborn son for the first time crashed over me and I would have killed to protect that little creature.

This is the sad bit – his mother had been hit by a car and had a broken back. Despite this she had tried to protect and keep her baby by dragging it along under her belly, grazing its little head and back until being captured. Unfortunately mom had to be put down – she was totally paralysed and badly hurt, but no one could bring themselves to put the baby down as well. So there she was for a day, before being taken to her next home, more of which I shall elaborate on later. Jenni left for a meeting, and I was left alone for what were to be some of the most amazing few hours of my life!

I was as scared as a first-time mom, wondering whether the baby would drink, whether she was in pain, if she was comfortable and of course how traumatised she must be feeling. Again I followed nature – I offered her the bottle frequently, because in the wild a baby would drink whenever it felt like it.

After two hours she realised that the bottle meant food, and as soon as I put it down on the table her little hands would reach out eagerly to grasp it! It was incredible and I could not get over how quickly she learnt! Curiosity got the better of her every now and then and she would tentatively grab the string on my jacket and give it a tug, quickly poking her head back under my arm when things got a bit much. I felt incredibly privileged to be given the chance to look after her – how many people do you know that have had the opportunity of holding and feeding a baby baboon?! It was one of the best days of my life.

Sadly, as I was becoming more and more attached to this precious little mite, it was time to leave and I parted from my little baby with the greatest reluctance. My only comfort was knowing that she would shortly be handed over to the best surrogate baboon mom, Nola Frazer, for eventual integration into a baboon troop of her very own.

Jenni Trethowan

The veterinarian that I have worked with the most is Dr Hernan Azorin. Dr Azorin has been helping with baboon emergencies for almost twenty years now and has had to deal with some horrific cases, but he has also experienced seeing the benefit of his hard work as the baboons return to their troop. This is Dr Azorin's story —

Many years ago at my practice, I was presented with my first baboon patient – and I must say it evoked some personal feelings in me.

First of all, something that still remains very present when I treat baboons is the fact that this is the closest I will ever come to treating a human, or more specifically because of their size, a child. Their hands so much resemble ours. Something which is quite profound to me, and which is not necessarily unique, is their eyes. They just emanate very special feelings of tenderness, depth and kindness – a very personal projection, I know.

When treating the babies, the task becomes a more personal involvement (especially having brought up my own children). The resemblance between baboons and ourselves is amplified dramatically.

I love treating baboons and they respond well to it. I suppose it is the closest I will come, as a vet, to the wildlife of Africa.

Without a doubt the hurts we have caused baboons are extreme: they have been shot, poisoned, trapped, run over – the list goes on. But in all the years that I have worked with the baboon conflict, I seldom come across instances of baboons wilfully hurting people. For sure, there have been some instances when people have been bitten by baboons, but usually those are cases when the situation has gotten out of hand – and in almost all situations it has been the ignorance of the human that created the friction. But this is not a competition, not about 'well the baboon did this or that' and 'deserves' what it gets.

This is about realising that intentionally hurting anyone, anything, for whatever reason, seldom solves anything. We need to start thinking of outsmarting the baboons, rather than hurting them, because so far the baboons are better at adapting to us than we have been at reacting to them.

It is not the strongest of the species that survives, nor the most intelligent, it is the one that is most adaptable to change...**Charles Darwin**

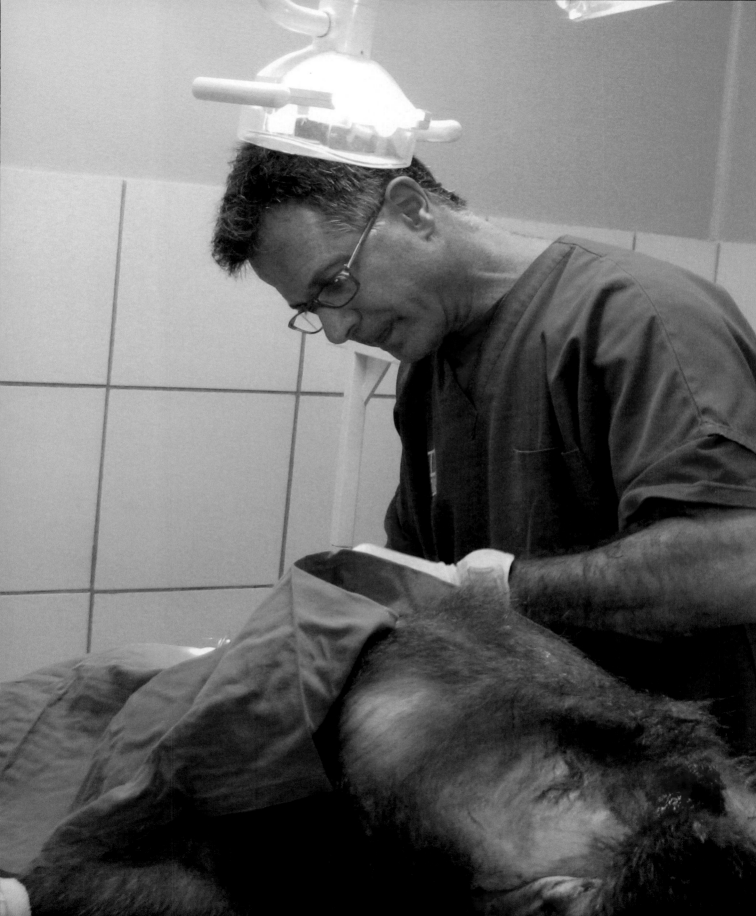

Chapter Seven

Primate encounters

"I lay flat on my back and looked up into the darkening sky. How sad it would be, I thought, if we humans ultimately were to lose all sense of mystery, all sense of awe. If our left brains were utterly to dominate the right so that logic and reason triumphed over intuition and alienated us absolutely from our innermost being, from our hearts, our souls." Jane Goodall

I had the honour of meeting Jane Goodall when she came to Cape Town in 2008. She is an exceptional public speaker and one of the most inspirational people I have met. Dr Goodall has carved a unique place in the world of science and academics, partly because she is a brilliant researcher, but mainly (I think) because she has not lost her sense of wonder or emotional response to the world. It was fantastic to meet a renowned scientist who recognises all animals as individuals with the right to names, not just as subject matter with codes. It encouraged me no end to hear how passionately she spoke of emotional issues, when all too often we are told to leave no room for intuition and feelings.

I have battled along a very lonely road in my efforts to get the plight of baboons recognised. I've been labelled more terms than I care to remember – mostly not very flattering. It took a very long time for me to accept that actually it is okay to be emotional. We have allowed negative emotions such as fear, hatred and anger to dominate a great many decisions that affected baboons, but when the ideals of ethics or love and generosity of spirit are mentioned, all too often scientists and decision makers become uncomfortable, and revert to cold fact.

I am so thrilled to see that slowly, bit by bit, it is becoming increasingly acceptable to talk about animals in terms of emotion or the loftier principles of ethics and values. We are starting to balance the cold facts with a bit of warmth that comes from doing 'the right thing'.

Lee Slabber

I was moved to tears by some of the stories that were sent to me for this book, but this story from Peter Cunningham had the most profound impact. I was awed by the fact that Peter entrusted me with his very personal experience, and also that he was prepared to have it included in my book.

Gomorra tangerines and the old lady
by Peter Cunningham

It was one of those laid-back Sunday afternoons only experienced on a farm when I was awoken by the noise. The cacophony that trashed my afternoon was caused by an old female baboon cornered in the chicken coop being beaten to death. She was in a bad way when I tore the staff off, thinking she would not see the approaching red Namibian sunset.

Phragmites reeds along the house dam offered her refuge and I tossed her some tangerines. With difficulty she ate them, discarding blood-stained peels while her piercing hazel eyes saw everything. A passing dove, an Oryx tossing its tail in the distance, leaves moving in the evening breeze – everything.

She lasted the night and during the following days I paid her my crepuscular visits, she awaiting my alms of tangerines and the eggs that had almost killed her. Visibly gaining strength with each visit, she eventually disappeared with the arrival of a passing troop. A week later she was back and we reinitiated our relationship.

One day as I passed her the eggs – broken in a dish as I had noticed that her teeth were broken and worn – she reached out towards me with eyes flitting between movements. Does she want to grab and bite me I thought? Staying still with bowl in hand, I waited to see what she intended doing. Her hairy brown arm and black leathery hand passed the bowl and gently took my left index finger and squeezed it whilst suddenly making lasting eye-contact. Here we were, hazel eyes and blue eyes, worldly and naive, in physical contact, a computer screen distance away from each other. Time stood still. The moment was too short – movement distracted her and she released me.

Many people I believe have profound life-changing moments, this was my epiphany. I have never put this incident to paper and have only told a handful of people, as undoubtedly this is one of those tales one tells with fear of being ridiculed as a baboon whisperer.

The following day whilst I was delayed on the farm, the old lady died – killed by the farm dogs whilst attempting to get to the tangerines in my garden. I buried her alone. The sun rises and sets and I have moved on, but often I still feel her and see that look, which touched me in more than one way.

It has been amazing to me how baboons seem to reach people when they most need it. I have seen lonely hurt people find solace in the quiet company of baboons. Just sitting on a rock in silence, watching the baboons get on with their lives, has in some mysterious way given soul-food to those in need.

The 'healing power of nature' is one of those esoteric topics that slowly is getting greater recognition, even acceptance. Perhaps, as Pastor James Grey suggests, it is because baboons are in harmony with God?

Bongwi the baboon

by James Grey

I met Bongwi on Monday afternoon on the narrow path that leads to the top of the Dragon's Spine above Fernkloof. I was huffing and puffing my way up the steep trail when he appeared before me blocking my path.

I stood still, hoping the sight of a shirtless human might frighten him away. Bongwi stood his ground. I smiled politely. He shimmied, feigning aggression, but his body language was unconvincing. Bongwi

wasn't in the mood for a showdown but he had no intention of letting me pass.

You should be careful when confronted by an unfriendly baboon. In the mountains we are the intruders. However, I didn't feel like doing an about-turn. I had climbed too high, and since I was in no hurry I decided to sit down and get to know my furry foe. We could chat about what it is like to be a baboon in a hostile world. We could talk about mountains.

Stories about living with baboons **96**

We could even speak about the God who reveals His glory in mountains. So that is what we did. High in the hills the baboon and the pastor sat 15 metres apart looking at each other and engaged in what I like to think was a conversation.

The conversation didn't exactly flow. There were too many distractions to keep Bongwi's mind focused. Besides, the constant war between man and baboon in this part of the world has not left the baboons well-disposed to talking to human beings about the meaning of life and especially about God. Memories run deep in the animal kingdom.

I tried nevertheless. I asked him about his family but that didn't create any spark of interest. I introduced the subject of the weather but that received a similar non-response. I played every pastoral card I could think of to ignite some rapport between us. I even thought of apologising for our unfriendliness when Bongwi and his family pop down for take-aways in Voelklip. That tactic didn't work either. He could smell insincerity as easily as a banana on my kitchen table.

And then something happened. At least, I like to think something happened. I asked Bongwi if he believed in God. He stared at me in that squinting way baboons do. Then he looked away to the mountains. Up and around he gazed, surveying the craggy rocks. I felt he had understood my question and that he was taking a few moments to consider the wonderful truth that for all the solitude of the landscape that he inhabited he was never alone; that Another walked with him, Someone who had made this gigantic cathedral of stone that surrounded us and whose presence and joy he felt as he climbed and leaped from rock to rock and ambled through the fynbos foraging for food.

Bongwi was soaking it all in. He seemed genuinely contented. This was his domain. This was where he worshipped his Creator and felt His immense strength. The mountains spoke to him of the power of his God, the fynbos of His beauty. The clean air was the exhilarating breath of the Spirit. This was Bongwi's home. This was Bongwi's church. Here was Bongwi's Lord.

Bongwi gazed down towards Voelklip then up towards Aasvoelkop. He looked at me intently and I could almost hear him say, "Why do you to want live down there when you have all this up here?" It was a telling question. I said nothing.

I don't think Bongwi liked me. I represented danger. Man, clever but ambiguous; light and darkness. Bongwi knows never to trust this creature that stands on two legs, who speaks harshly using rude words. He refuses to believe that such a cruel creature was made in the image of God. He prefers to be left alone to enjoy his mountains and his Creator.

Jenni Trethowan

This is the wisdom of the Ape
Who yelps beneath the Moon —
'Tis God who made me in His shape
He is a Great Baboon.
'Tis He who tilts the moon askew
Provide him his trapeze;
And fans the forest trees,
The heavens which are broad and blue
He swings with tail divinely bent
Around those azure bars
And munches to his soul's content
The kernels of the stars;
And when I die, His loving care
Will raise me from the sod
To learn the perfect Mischief there
The Nimbleness of God.

Roy Campbell

One of my personal battles is in dealing with the issue of classifying baboon 'feelings' as anthropomorphic. It is obvious to me that baboons have very clear feelings and emotions, and often these emotions are displayed on their very expressive faces. This moving contribution from Erica Klocke illustrates my thoughts on the subject—

An incident which was very poignant occurred late one afternoon. I was in a large bus when we spotted a large troop coming towards us, crossing over the veld towards the mountain. Lagging far behind was a lone female, limping. She seemed to limp first on one side then on the other. As she came closer, we saw that she was carrying a limp, very young baby in her paws. Possibly it had been knocked by a car or bitten by a snake. About 10 metres from us, she sat down in the road and started rubbing or massaging the baby while uttering a pitiful moaning sound, then stopping and actually blowing air into the baby's mouth, trying to resuscitate the little one.

About four weeks later, I was in the park again and came across a large troop again and there was a female, the same size as the one we had been watching, now carrying with her the totally dried-out remains of a little baby. It could have been the same baboon we had been watching before. I will never forget that sad face and the desperate attempts to revive her baby.

Erica Klocke

Jenni Trethowan

Brett Cole

A tank of baboons

by Patrick Dowling, Wildlife and Environment Society SA

The origin of the expression a barrel of monkeys may be clouded in the mists of time, but if anyone asks where a tank of baboon comes from, this is where.

Early in the 21st Century when the Norbertine fathers on the Kommetjie hillside had recently decided that the intensive and hydroponic cultivation of tomatoes was not for them any more and that therefore the large ten thousand litre green plastic water tank could take a rest from its primary function, a curious young baboon, nameless to humans but not to the troop who were regular and

not altogether shriven visitors to this historical and holy place, bethought itself to investigate the receptacle more closely as is the wont of the youth in their quest for knowledge and experience. Risk is an essential part of this.

Perhaps there was an overestimation of personal jumping ability; perhaps there was underestimation of tank height and internal lack of purchase. The need for lesson-learning and juice-stewing may even have been part of the collective primatoid psyche. The exact reason is not quite clear and no slip, jump or push was recorded.

The tank, having been for a while empty of its iron-rich pumped water, was now partly full of our immature cousin in an agitated and expressive condition.

Now the Norbertines, while not like Trappists or Carmelites who take vows of silence, do not celebrate noise and rowdy behaviour, except at fund-raising bingo evenings. So the loud activities and utterances from the green tank near the library section of the monastery caused brother Neil and his confreres as much anxiety and distress as felt by the rocking tank's inmate. Hastily brother Neil looked through the list of paid-up parishioners, scanning for one that might fall into the wildlife rescue category.

A short prayer to Saint Anthony may have helped produce this writer's name, but so it was, and armed with rope, ladder and limited knowledge of baboons he set out to answer this call of nature. Jenni joined him at the denoument as the now rusty dusty red and more seasoned baboon, having swarmed up the knotted rope with great rapidity and disdain for his liberators, now loped off to join the rest of the troop somewhere on Slangkop.

Brett Cole

Brett Cole

One of my favourite Welcome Glen residents is surely **Allyson Vine**. Allyson and her late husband Fritz had a wonderful relationship with the baboons, they never encouraged or fed the baboons, and the baboons just know they are not allowed in the house. But Allyson takes pure delight in watching the baboons in her garden or as they walk along the road. Allyson has the uncanny knack of sending me a baboon story whenever I am at a low ebb, and inevitably her tales delight and bring a smile – and remind me why I do what I do. This is an excerpt from a typical email from Allyson –

I have just been watching the baboons. I got up because I heard a typical kiddies' fight...gosh but they know how to screech and perform! They were next door in the neighbour's waterberry tree. I'm sure the scrap was over the fruit. Then one came up our driveway with a pine cone and they ran down right past me, under the back of the car, up through the garden and over the fence.

As I stood there watching I noticed a youngster up against the retaining wall behind a planter, his little fingers holding onto the top of the wall above him. As I realised he was hiding there I saw another one creep up alone above him. I was thrilled to see they were playing hide and seek. Four of them ran onto our grassy pavement, with its gentle slope. They love to play there, rolling down and doing somersaults and having a general rough and tumble.

Today once more I give thanks for the pleasure these wonderful baboons bring into our lives. I think it is a real privilege having them cross over our fence and wander about so close to us. It really lifts the vibrations having something to bring laughter and delight to us so often.

How right Allyson is – if we can just remember to laugh and take delight in the good moments, it will surely make the bad moments easier to bear. It is a well-accepted fact that our human wiring enables us to remember the good times a lot more easily than the bad, we will remember pleasure rather than pain. So, as Cher Pozanovich describes below, a joyous moment can stay with you for a long, long time –

My favourite Sunday treat is getting into the mountains on my bike. Tokai is particularly enjoyable as the leg-burning uphills are quenched with the last remaining pine forests and the exquisite panoramic views. I am not the fastest rider and so often stay behind to breathe in the echo of the mountain and bask in the joy of being immersed in nature.

Sightings of the Tokai baboon troop have always been a delight. I adore the way they sit in the road watching us pass, as if they were watching a TV show – I can almost hear them saying "I'll bet 20 berries on him!" But seriously, for me just seeing them in their natural environment is magnificent.

One particular Sunday as I neared a scenic hill site I heard a lady screaming in panic. And when I approached the scene I saw that an English couple had laid out a picnic to delight in the view – but of course the smell of that camembert and fresh bread got not only my mouth watering but attracted a whole troop of excitable baboons. They came running with excitement. I then told the couple to pack away their food and walk away, as the baboons were certainly not after them but the delicious aroma of their delights.

When I saw they were safely away I got back on my bike to continue my ride, but just then the most incredible thing happened that will stay with me forever – as one of the male patriarchs and a few of his mates nibbled on the crumbs left by tourists, a little baby baboon came skipping towards me with a yellow flower in her hand and what looked like a smile on her face. I felt as if she was displaying the most beautiful expression of gratitude and freedom that I had ever seen.

Now she did not hand me the flower, which I had hoped for, but I can tell you that I keep the memory of that joyous spirit in my heart for always.

Lee Slabber

The way in which **Jean Prior** described her moment with baboons was so emotive that I could see the baboons and dogs. What a wonderful moment in time –

"A shower of rain had just fallen. I looked outside and, to my surprise, saw three huge adult baboons stretched up on their hind legs, doing what looked like a ballet dance, stretching, leaping and pirouetting high up into the air.

My two little dogs raced across towards them with me in hot pursuit yelling for them to come back as I was afraid they would be killed. Next thing to my amazement I saw the dogs performing in the same manner. Flying Ants were billowing from the earth! The animals were having a good feast!"

Life is too short to rush through. By taking time to delight in the world around us and keep our sense of wonder, we will be better able to cope with the tough times that are as much a part of life as the good. Baboons have the ability to 'just get on with life', they work hard and rest well, and have their soap-opera dramas with friendships and fights.

Perhaps the greatest gift baboons can give us is that, if we can take the time to watch their antics with amusement, we will gain a fragile bubble of joy, a wonderful emotion that lightens the spirit and – as Allyson says – 'lifts the vibrations.'

The life I touch for good or ill will touch another
life, and that in turn another, until who knows
where the trembling stops or in what far place my
touch will be felt – **Frederick Beuchner**

Chapter Eight

Touched by a baboon

There are certain individuals who touch our lives. Sometimes they stay in our lives, but often they are part of a passing moment, a brief interlude in time, yet we remember those individuals forever. Frequently the individuals are teachers, not necessarily teachers in the academic sense, but teachers nonetheless. Sometimes we are not aware of any lesson or epiphany until years later when we may perhaps look back at our memories and realise what the true meaning of that encounter was. But sometimes those brief encounters are merely that – a special moment in time.

In my years working with the baboons there have been individual animals whose character, personality or mere presence has made them stand out. It could be argued that anthropomorphic emotionalism clouds thinking and creates overly-sentimental 'bunny huggers' – or in this case 'baboon huggers' – sometimes we do need special moments to make us feel – and then think.

Some of the stories sent to me demonstrate a huge emotional response to certain situations where individual baboons touched peoples' lives in a meaningful way.

The best known baboon of recent times has surely got to be Eric Baboon. He is something of a living legend and it is not for nothing that the monitors call Eric 'the genius'. They think he is the most intelligent and cunning of all baboons. Despite Eric giving the monitors a real run-around, the men have a high regard for the old man of the mountains and when he was injured, a few of the monitors made a point of visiting him in hospital. There are enough stories about this 'great ape' to warrant a book dedicated purely to Eric's escapades, but until I can get all those stories together, here are a couple to introduce you to this remarkable baboon.

One call I particularly enjoyed was from someone wanting to book a walk with the baboons. The woman asked me, "Will we be able to see Eric?" I explained the situation and asked her why she particularly wanted to see Eric. Her answer had me in stitches as she said that she had a particular connection with Eric, in fact he had been at her wedding and appeared in many of the wedding photographs. It seems that Eric had been on one of his lone raiding sprees and decided that the wedding spread was too good an attraction to pass by.

Luckily the bride retained a sense of humour and rather than feeling her special day was ruined, she reasoned that it was part and parcel of living on the peninsula.

Wally Petersen and I started KEAG together in 1990, but prior to that Wally had spent many months observing the troop on Slangkop Mountain, so he had, over the years, built up a great connection with Eric. Here is Wally's tale of Eric the King —

I first met Eric in the early nineties when I was following the Slangkop baboon troop as part of my studies. At that time he was not yet the leader of the troop, but he was a strikingly handsome young male and he moved with confidence and grace. I had been struggling to get close to the troop but it had progressively got easier and I had a feeling that the troop would soon accept me.

Slangkop Mountain had recently had a fire and I was able to follow the troop on my mountain bike. On this specific day I spent a short while trying to find the troop and eventually came across them close to the blockhouse. I got off my bicycle and walked slowly towards them.

When I was fairly close I climbed onto a rock about one metre in diameter and sat down to make observations. Eric looked over in my direction and then came trotting over straight towards me. I was not sure quite what to do and decided just to stay on the rock and not back off. Eric jumped up onto a rock about three metres in front of mine. We sat and stared at each other; I admiring this handsome young animal that one day would be the leader of the troop and king of Slangkop, and Eric, well, he was looking at this strange bearded apparition with binoculars and camera hanging from its neck.

He would look at me and then glance away as if he could not quite believe what he was seeing. Then suddenly he seemed to make up his mind and in two jumps he was on the ground and jumping onto my rock. I got such a fright that I stepped backwards forgetting that there was nothing behind me. I went crashing to the ground with binoculars and camera flying. I lay on my back trying to get my wind back and glanced up to see Eric looking down at me. He looked for all the world as if he was trying to suppress laughter.

After that incident it was if the troop decided that I certainly posed no threat to them and I was able to spend many happy months following them around. It took many years before I was able to get my revenge on Eric. He had now become the leader of the troop and they had taken to the occasional raiding of houses. I got a call at the Kommetjie Environmental Awareness Group offices where I worked. Apparently the baboon troop had gained access into a house in Misty Cliffs, and were having a jolly good time.

When I got to the house I could see that the owners must have left a big sliding window open. I walked up quietly and peeked into the house. The sight that greeted me was unforgettable. It was a large open-plan room with the kitchen separated from the lounge only by a wooden counter. Inside were at least ten baboons ranging from Eric to small babies. Some sat on the couch in a very leisurely and laidback fashion, others were on the wooden counter with their hands in cereal boxes. It was a banquet of note. The fridge door was open and the contents dispersed amongst the raiders, but what was most striking and amusing was the fact that they had obviously all taken turns to lick at the tub of butter. Each and every animal had a yellow nose and mouth, it was hilarious.

After enjoying this strange spectacle for a short while I realised that I had better try to get them out of the house. I climbed through the window but they all immediately ran down the corridor and into the bedrooms. Making sure that I was not seen I slipped into the pantry and pulled the door closed only leaving an inch gap through which I could peep. After a little while they all came back into the kitchen to resume their feast. They were now between me and the window, perfect.

I threw the door open and gave a cry and flapped my arms wildly. It worked! They got a huge fright and immediately went scampering for the window. I had out-babooned them and the last baboon out was Eric. He looked back at me with a quizzical look on his face and I did my best to suppress my laughter.

In 2008 Eric was mauled by three dogs in Kommetjie and nobody was sure whether he would survive the horrific wounds. I sat next to him whilst we waited for the people to arrive to dart him. So many thoughts went through my mind, we had shared the same mountain for twenty years and I had watched him grow and now age with such dignity and grace. There was something unique about him. The baboon monitors have no doubt that he is the smartest baboon they have ever met. I wondered if this was the end of his time; in a way it was quite fitting in that he had been mauled trying to protect his family. Eric the Brave!

At the same time I felt that this ending would not befit the way he had lived. He needed to die naturally on Slangkop Mountain where he had lived for so long. I lay on the ground and stared into his eyes, or should I say eye, as by now only one was fully functioning. We looked at each other, and I swear I saw a flicker of recognition, but I also saw a flicker of life and the will to live. Right then I knew he was going to survive his wounds.

A week later we let Eric go on Slangkop Mountain. Whilst he was in the cage I took the chance to grab his hand and shake it, in a way to thank him for his friendship and to acknowledge the fact that knowing him had enriched my life. We opened the cage door. Eric (still slightly drugged) came out of the cage, bent down and sniffed the ground – for all the world kissing the earth – and then did the most perfect forward roll before getting up and slowly walking up the hill. He was back on his beloved Slangkop Mountain.

LONG LIVE ERIC,
LONG LIVE ERIC THE KING!

Eric, old man of the mountain...

Jenni Trethowan

But if Eric is the king and urban legend – then Jane Baboon must be the connoisseurs' choice. Janey, who featured in Chapter 3, is a subordinate girl from Eric's troop – one of the most remarkable little baboons I have known. Jane does not stay with the troop. When she is about to give birth, she leaves the troop and comes into the villages of Kommetjie and Scarborough where she keeps a quiet life, managing to stay under the radar so that the majority of residents don't even know she is there, but a select few do enjoy her presence.

Jane was very well-known in Kommetjie. A favourite haunt was the local hairdressing salon where Jane would spend hours gazing in the window, perhaps longing for a cut, wash and blow? Jane also visited Dee French and Margie Armstrong on a regular basis, as she slept in the mountains directly above their homes. Here is a reminiscence from Margie –

Chris Cole

I remember a summer's day in 2005 when Richard had invited some business people round for drinks and a braai. I had just finished watching Jane's regular daily grooming session. I greeted everyone while Richard fixed the drinks. I looked up and saw Jane sitting on the ledge above our sliding doors, eyeing out these strangers. I reassured everyone that she didn't bite and that she was actually rather a civilized baboon and they carried on chatting and drinking and began to relax.

After a while she lay down and tried to sleep but one eye kept opening, checking on what was going on. Eventually she decided to stretch and she turned to face the wall, her tail over the edge. I looked in horror as I realized what was about to happen and the man standing below was even more horrified as the stream of urine drenched him and watered his drink down. His wife was disgusted and a stream of insults about wild beasts poured from the red lips and I realized she was not the sort of person I would welcome again into my home. The other people were laughing as Jane slid down from the roof and shuffled down the stairs to the pool for a drink of water. She looked back once and as I caught her gaze I could have sworn she had a smirk on her face.

When Jenni asked me to write a few words on Jane, I wondered, what can I say about her, this grey-haired bandy-legged creature with the yellow teeth who wormed her way into my heart and soul and then mysteriously disappeared when I left to go to my home in Ireland for 3 weeks in January 2007. I can only say I miss you terribly. **Margie Armstrong**

D.Bosman

Jane spent a great deal of time in Scarborough with her first baby and I used to get many calls from residents to report Jane asleep in the kitchen, or on the patio – but this story from **Xandra** of Scarborough was priceless –

Having lived my life between Tokai and Scarborough, baboon encounters are inevitable, with the baboons definitely being ahead of the game. The score, if I were to keep one, would be: baboon 50 - myself 0. However, my favourite baboon story is not about one of these, in this particular encounter no scores were kept, no points taken.

I have a good friend, Tim, who I met many years ago in the UK. In late January 2003 he fulfilled a promise to visit me in Cape Town – his first trip ever to South Africa. He arrived late one night after a long flight and the following morning, when I suggested a walk up the mountain behind my house in Scarborough, he was quick to pass in favour of a snooze in the hammock on the balcony.

When I returned a few hours later, I was astonished to find Tim fast asleep in the hammock with a baby baboon passed out on his chest and the mother asleep underneath the hammock. Tim, never having seen a baboon before, did not know how to react when the pair moved in.

The baby was not shy at all and climbed all over him demanding attention before eventually falling asleep. Tim was enchanted with the baby and the mother didn't seem to mind. However, I explained that contact between humans and baboons is not encouraged. I was personally very relieved that the visitors hadn't discovered my kitchen.

Apparently Jane, the mother, had left the Scarborough troop when the father of her baby had been replaced as leader, rightly concerned that the new leader would kill her baby.

I never saw her again and I can only hope that all went well with them both, the gentlest, best-mannered baboons I have ever had the pleasure of meeting, and definitely the high point of Tim's visit.

Yet another Jane story came in from Kommetjie icon **Gary van Rooyen**. Gary is a well-known sportsman who has achieved great success as an athlete, yet he says this particular run was a highlight for him.

Isn't it amazing how sometimes you are just in the right place at the right time?

It was one of those magnificent Kommetjie evenings – yes, the ones that only us privileged Kommetjie locals have come to savour and enjoy.

I was off on my sunset run over Slangkop and just rounded the first corner when I saw Janey coming up over the edge. She was all alone, but hardly skitterish of me running by. As much as my objective is always to push hard up the hill so as to ease off and enjoy the down run on the other side, the opportunity and serenity of the situation just looked too good to pass up. I slowed down to a walk. The wind had abated, the sun was setting and the ocean was in all its splendour. Anyway, I was feeling like I needed company and someone to chat to.

What transpired next was truly an experience that I will forever cherish. Janey took one glance at me (probably liked my shorts!) and promptly fell into rhythm with my walk. I introduced myself, mentioned that I had been surfing and jogging in the area for 30-odd years and that she and her family had occasionally caused a bit of havoc in my house on the mountainside. She kept glancing at me with interest and was absolutely intrigued with my company and conversation. We were so close, we could have held hands. Other than stopping to prise a squashed banana peel off the tarmac, Janey kept with me all the way to the top, pausing momentarily for a photo shoot for some tourist along the way. We eventually parted company at the crest after a memorable 10 minute interlude that still brings a smile to my face.

PS – she did mention that they really meant no harm and seeing that we had come and built in their area and eradicated their food supply, surely they could pop down for the odd scrap.

Chris Cole

One of the aspects of baboons that few people talk about or acknowledge in any way is the incredible role baboons have played in the field of medicine. For years doctors and scientists practised on baboons and, sadly, in too many medical institutions to mention, baboons are still held captive and experimented on for the 'benefit of mankind'.

I recently met four victims of medical research, four female baboons who had spent their entire lives in cages, subjected to regular tests in the forms of injections and vaccinations. Their tattooed legs and desperate eyes were such a grim reminder of holocaust victims that I always thought of these poor creatures as the 'Auschwitz girls'. Their lives had little joy or happiness. Probably their eventual passing was the greatest relief they had. I mention them deliberately as I don't want their sad lives to go unnoticed, unmarked in any way. They gave greatly and are remembered as they were named: Blanche, Rose, Dorothy and Sophia – Golden Girls each one.

The vivisection debate is always highly emotive as the lives of individual animals are discounted against the benefits to humanity. I am not going to get into that debate here, suffice to raise the issue for you to contemplate further in your own way.

One person who has direct experience of the role baboons have played in medical research is Dale Fox. Here is her account of an incredible experience –

'Pump off'. The words were always loaded with anticipation. The heart continued to beat on its own, pink and pulsating with the age-old rhythm of life. The rest would be fairly routine – if one could call this particular case routine. The cannulae would be removed, the loose ends tied up, after which the Prof would pull off his gloves and leave the assistants to close the chest and see the patient off to the ICU. It had all been done so many times before. Yet this case was different. My memory is slightly clouded by time, but I recall very well that when I left the cardiac theatre in the early hours of that morning, I passed a patient trolley in the theatre annex. There was a bunny blanket covering a body – unusual, because bodies were never left unattended in passages.

However, I knew full well why this particular body was lying unattended, in death, waiting to be fetched. I pulled back the bunny blanket, and looked down at the peaceful face – the chest stitched closed, the hairy limbs lying flaccid at the sides. This body would be returned to the animal lab later that day – the body of a baboon whose heart had been harvested to save a patient in dire need of a heart transplant.

The baboon heart would, it was hoped, buy the patient a little time, until a suitable human donor could be found. I recall that the patient did not, in fact survive. But we had tried.

Not long after that I left the Cardiac Team to take up business interests in a totally opposite direction to what I had been trained for, and although I often thought about my time as a member of Prof. Chris Barnard's team, I never imagined what an impact my 'baboon experiences' as part of that team would have on me many years later.

I have always been an avid hiker and nature lover, and have encountered baboons in the wild on many occasions. But I was not prepared for one of the most amazing encounters of my life – which occurred some 25 years after I had left the Cardiac Team.

A friend and I went to Barrydale in the Western Cape one weekend in July 2004, prompted by a mutual friend to go to experience the full-moon labyrinth walk at The Manger – also known as the Joshua Baboon Rehabilitation Centre, run by two most amazing souls, Dr Peter Frazer and his wife Nola. It was our first labyrinth walk, and we were so inspired by the entire experience that we asked Nola if we could return the following day to see the owls in daylight, as I have a special interest in owls.

The following day we were graciously received, and spent time with the owls, who (I use 'who' rather than 'which', as they are also sentient beings) had also been injured or traumatized, and were being rehabilitated for release. Then Nola mentioned to my friend Wilma that she had been informed that Wilma worked in the energy healing field, as a Body Talk practitioner, and that a very special baboon, Oliver, had severe epileptic attacks which, she was told, could be helped by Body Talk.

That was the beginning of one of the most special periods in our lives. Wilma was so overcome that she immediately agreed to give Oliver Baboon a session – the first of many, which saw him recover to the extent that he hardly ever had fits anymore.

While Wilma was giving Oliver his session, Nola took me to meet Njelo Baboon: magnificent, regal, with an aura of immense power, Njelo Baboon. Not just baboon power – that he certainly had, as an adult male Chacma baboon, who had been alpha male of his own troop. But Njelo Baboon's power was something I had never experienced before - this was a power which penetrated all layers of resistance, piercing the heart, with an overwhelming sense of love.

The irony of all this is that Njelo Baboon was blind – thanks to the inhumanity of man. Something profound happened to me that day. In the presence of this awesome baboon something was triggered, the memory of a baboon who had sacrificed his life for a human so long ago. I broke down and wept like a child. I, the strong, in-control, unemotional egotistical human being that I was, no longer had any control of my emotions. Nola kindly explained that he really was fine, and that although he appeared somewhat disfigured, he had healed completely. However, my reaction went much deeper than that. I explained to Nola the role I had played all those years ago, as a member of 'The Team' and that not only baboons had been involved, but chimpanzees as well – as sacrifices for human life. And so began Njelo's and my mutual healing of each other, at a level so deep that our story appeared on SABC 3's 'Healing power of nature'. And heal I did, gaining at the same time a deeper understanding of how animals view their role in the greater scheme of things, in which humans are but small role-players, yet manage to have such astounding effects, both positive and negative.

From Njelo Baboon I learnt about acceptance, surrender – not as in giving up, but as in surrendering to the ebb and flow of life, over which we have no control – about the necessity for paradox in life, for without an acceptance and understanding of polarity/duality, there can be no existence.

The most profound experience I have ever had in my life was sitting in the enclosure with Njelo Baboon, while, just as a blind human would, he gently examined my hands, and then my entire face, finally placing his hands behind my head and drawing me closer, so that our faces touched. It was an acknowledgement of our interconnectedness with all that is on this beautiful planet.

I salute all of nature, and especially my brother in nature, Njelo Baboon. You have taught me more about consciousness and mindfulness than I could ever have learnt on my own.

Not forgetting all the other marvelous baboons at The Joshua Baboon Rehab Centre – who all, in their own way, teach so many lessons, to all who are willing to learn.

Brett Cole

Angelina Ballerina

by Wynter Worsthorne

Her skull was fractured in three places causing her to be temporarily blind and to twirl in slow circles when attempting to move, hence the name Angelina Ballerina. I got to know Angelina during her recovery period, when she crept into all of our hearts.

It took six weeks for her to fully recover and when she felt completely ready we took her back to her natal troop of Da Gama Park.

She'd only been back with them for a few days when I got a frantic phone call from Jenni saying that they couldn't find Angelina — there had been a terrible storm the night before and we were worried.

I tried to see if I could get a sense of where she was and the moment I tuned into Angelina's energy I got an image of her happily playing on the mountain with the troop. That was odd, and although it felt completely right, it didn't match up with the fact that she wasn't with her troop, and I doubted myself.

Whilst helping Jenni search for her, I kept getting the same images and the feeling that Angelina was quite okay and happy. A few days later, an ecstatic Jenni called to tell me that Angelina had been found. Unexpectedly, she was with the Kommetjie troop (Eric's troop), sticking with a young male and a couple of juveniles her own age.

Over the months we saw Angelina growing and playing and interacting as if she'd been born into the troop. It was a joy to see.

My second experience with Angelina did not have such a happy ending. She was one of the three juveniles poisoned with a Dieldrin cocktail, wittingly or unwittingly (we will never know for sure) put out where the baboons could ingest it.

The first two baboons we found died at the vet shortly after arriving. Angelina took three days to die. Once again Jenni took her home to care for her. It was awful to see her convulsing and in such pain, but we hoped against hope that she would pull through, after all she had done so before, against all odds. It was not to be and Angelina died in Jenni's arms.

A few days after that Jenni herself fell ill. I was terrified when I noticed exactly the same symptoms I had seen in Angelina in my dear friend. Jenni eventually recovered, but not before she had experienced the exact pain and suffering that Angelina had endured.

Ironically, through Jenni's physical ordeal, the awareness of the plight of the Peninsula baboons increased. People around the world started wanting to help. Together brave Angelina Ballerina and my equally brave friend changed perceptions and through their suffering made people realise how much help our furry cousins need.

There are so many more stories where people have been touched in a deep and utterly profound way by baboons. The truth is that it is not our touching an animal that has significance, but it is in allowing the animal to touch our lives and souls that we can become healed in some small way.

The beautiful stories included in this chapter all reflect the way in which an individual baboon had a profound effect on the human involved. Those individuals are all known and have names. Naming baboons is yet another controversial aspect of the baboon world. Some scientists do name the animals they work with, such as Jane Goodall who named David Greybeard, Flo and Flint, Spindle and Mel; or Robert Salpolsky who used wonderful biblical names like Solomon, Rachel and Job to identify the members of the troops he worked with. However many other scientists prefer to categorise their subject matter with codes – a more clinical approach.

Is it more emotive to 'name' the animals? Names acknowledge the individuals and emphasise their unique qualities, so it is probably true that we are more likely to form attachments or develop feelings for those we know, those who are named.

Animals are individual sentient beings with feelings and emotional responses. They are individuals, not collectives – no more than we are. Named or not.

If I was gifted and could properly understand baboon communications, maybe I would know their true names, but in the meantime I acknowledge their individuality and I hope that the names the monitors and I give them are not insulting to them, but acceptable choices as we go through our learning together.

I have not named all of the baboons (I don't know all of them well enough), but I do have deep love for each and every baboon regardless of whether they are named or not. The gifts they have given are profound, I take joy in those gifts and feel sorrow at each of their passing.

Chris Cole

If all the beasts were gone, man would die from
a great loneliness of spirit — **Chief Seattle**

Jenni Trethowan

Silly Old Baboon

There was a Baboon
who, one afternoon,
said "I think I will fly to the sun."
So, with two great palms
strapped to his arms,
he started his take-off run.
Mile after mile
he galloped in style
but never once left the ground.
"You're running too slow"
said a passing crow,
"Try reaching the speed of sound."
So he put on a spurt —
by God how it hurt!
the soles of his feet caught fire.
There were great clouds of steam
as he raced through a stream
but he still didn't get any higher.
Racing on through the night
both his knees caught alight
and smoke billowed out from his rear.
Quick to his aid
came a fire brigade
who chased him for over a year.
Many moons passed by.
Did Baboon ever fly?
Did he ever get to the sun?
I've just heard today
That he's well on his way!
He'll be passing through Acton at one.

P.S. Well, what did you expect from a Baboon?

Spike Milligan

Unless someone like you cares a whole awful lot,
nothing is going to get better. It's not.

From 'The Lorax' by Dr Seuss

Chapter Nine

Stories from children

If one of the recurring themes throughout this book is that your behaviour will affect how the baboons respond in any given situation, then another of the recurring themes must surely be – keep a sense of humour! Spike Milligan's wonderful verse does just that, and that laughter and lightness underline yet another recurring theme – balance! So many times it has been fear and anger which cloud judgement, but above all else we need to keep a balance.

One of the biggest fears that I encounter is from parents who fear that baboons might attack their child, or most commonly: "Are we going to wait for a child to be killed before we do anything?"

I would never discount the fears that the parents express: anything that you feel is very real to you, and often not without just cause. But we have to allow that our fears can affect our children negatively; we set patterns that could dominate our children's future so it is so important to try to retain some objectivity and see the situation for what it is – rather than what it could be.

As an example of what I am trying to express, I would like to retell a tale from my own childhood.

As a child growing up in what is now Zimbabwe, I remember vividly watching those dramatic electric storms with my mother. She would point out the lightning patterns and the different sounds of thunder claps, and I remember standing entranced, drinking it all in. To this day, I love to sit in the dark watching thunder storms.

It was only fairly recently that I learned my mother was in fact terrified of thunder and lightning, but she didn't want me to be. So she found the drama, the colours, the sounds and she focused on those. She kept me entranced, hid her fear and gave me a gift. My mom is amazing, but sadly I did not inherit her bravery. I am terrified of frogs. I could not summon any courage to hide this from my children, they know it but luckily it did not scar them – they find it humorous. What we teach our children will set patterns in their lives and down the line.

I would hate anyone reading this to think that I am trying to preach a 'huggy, feely' attitude to baboons – not at all! Baboons are sentient wild animals. Treat them with respect and caution, and do not invade their space any more than you would that of a stranger at the mall. Do not tease them, as you would not tease the rottweiler on the corner. Do not hurt them, as you would not intentionally hurt anything or anyone. The simple rules are the best rules and I hope that by parents retaining a sense of right and wrong, humour and caution, we will learn how to best teach our children.

I think that it may well be appropriate to compare some of the behaviour of baboons to that of unruly children, and then ask yourself – how do you deal with your own children, your grandchildren?

Generally, firmness without being violent, and clear boundaries with no mixed signals (so, sorry to say, NO, you cannot put down grain for the guinea fowl and expect the baboons NOT to eat it). Most of the rules that apply to raising your children can be applied to baboons.

But all the above is from an adult point of view. Children have a refreshing view on things, and I hope never to lose sight of what children think! Here are a few comments that certainly made me smile and think a while!

The Taylor children sent me wonderfully pragmatic narrations of the same incident –

When I lived in Malawi my mum told me to not go near the baboons because they could scratch you to pieces. So I felt scared of baboons when I saw them in Cape Town. Imagine how I felt when I was caught up a tree in Kommetjie with a baboon on the same branch!

One sunny day I was at 'Fishermans' climbing a tree. A big fluffy black thing that looked like a dog came running out of the restaurant straight towards me. But then I knew it was a baboon. It jumped onto the tree and sat next to me!! I jumped down and hurt my ankle. But I am not scared of baboons anymore

because it did not scratch me at all. The only thing that hurt was my ankle and I did that myself.
Jack Taylor, age 7

And now Emily's version –

Have you ever been touched by a baboon? Shall I tell you about the time I was? Well I was climbing a tree behind my brother Jack at the Fisherman's play-ground in Kommetjie. Jack turned around and then he jumped off the tree suddenly. I thought he had jumped down because he had heard my mum calling him. But then I felt something tap me lightly on my shoulder. It felt like a small child, it was so gentle. I thought it must be somebody else climbing the tree. I turned around and saw something that was not small at all! A large brown dog? No, a BABOON! I didn't really have time to think. I half slid, half jumped out of the tree and ran quickly to the table that my mum was sitting at! It was such a shock to realise I had been touched by a baboon!
Emily Taylor, age 9

Interestingly, three of the stories sent to me were from Taylor children, but only two of them are related. Ashley Taylor of Kommetjie sent through her tales of baboon woe –

Once upon a time we went to Buffelsbaai and a baboon walked up to me and smelt me and touched me. I had to kneel down and not look in the baboon's eyes. Do you know the reason why? It's because if you look them in their eyes, they will think that you want to fight!

And once I was supposed to be sleeping, but I wasn't and I heard the door of the fridge opening and smashing closed. So then I came out of my room, and I went upstairs and the female baboon was on the stairs. I screamed like my leg was cut off. I ran upstairs and sat by Franko. Mummy ran downstairs and Grandpa was in the house already. Grandpa chased the male baboon out of the house, and then Grandpa turned around and the female was behind him. Then Franko and me came downstairs. Big mess, tjo! There was watermelon on the floor, lots of smashed eggs on the floor. I got such a shock that I had hot water and sugar to settle me down.

Ashley Taylor

It was as a result of the first experience in the house that Ashley's grandpa Simon took her on a baboon walk. He wanted to assuage some of the negative effects that the encounter left on Ashley. She very much enjoyed seeing the fascinating creatures in their natural habitat, on their own ground.

Hugo Hulsman describes his baboon encounter, and makes a plea for greater tolerance –

My baboon story started in Rooi Els. We were sitting in our lounge, we being me, my mom, my sister and some friends of ours. My dog Goya was put in the back of the car so he could not run away, for the house had no fences. A moment later we heard an 'Oooo!' sound. My mom thought it was Goya jumping through the stable door. She looked around and saw a huge male baboon. Everyone ran outside, except Isabella my sister who was jumping on the couch. A moment later she saw it but she was so scared she couldn't move. I thought the baboon was going to take her away. My mom ran in and picked up Isabella and got outside with me again. All the baboon took was a loaf of bread and some apples.

My dad came to pick us up to take us home and my mom was going to stay in Rooi Els. My other dog Daisy, our Jack Russell, was running and barking. We saw her come out of the bush chasing a big baboon. My mom thought she would come round to the back of the house and find a head over here and a body over here. Thankfully my dad went round and caught Daisy. A few days later my mom was still in Rooi Els and we were in Cape Town. When we got back, my mom told me that she was sitting on the veranda and a baboon ran past her and into the house. To get it out, my mom threw tea at it and it ran right away. So that's the end of my baboon story.

Please don't hurt baboons, they can be pains but we are sometimes worse, like the fires on the mountains, poisoning them and shooting at them. Learn more about baboons and you will find they are very kind and gentle, but don't take any chances.

Hugo Hulsman

One of the most incredible experiences I have ever had was when a concerned mom asked me to take her very traumatized daughter to walk with the baboons. The family has a holiday home in Pringle Bay, and they had had some very scary experiences – understandably the daughter was petrified. I hate the idea of children growing up terrified of anything, let alone baboons, so I welcomed the opportunity to take the mother and daughter to walk on their own with the baboons.

We kept some distance from the baboons and I was able to point out the various aspects of baboon behaviour and explain what was happening. Baboons have such an interesting social dynamic – a bit like a soap opera really – and soon the youngster found herself caught up watching the adults grooming and the antics of the juveniles. Gradually she relaxed and even started to laugh at the goings-on of baboon life. I was delighted to have been able to help balance the frights with the other side of baboons.

There will be times when baboons see easily-available food and want to snatch it for themselves. There will be times when fights break out amongst members of the troop, fights that have nothing to do with us, but which are very frightening to see. But if we can teach our children not to tease the baboons and to leave them alone; not to try to hurt them and above all not to confront baboons over food – then I can see no instance where a baboon would choose to hurt your child.

In my home village of Kommetjie, the local primary school has baboons coming onto the property on a regular basis. The school has had to practise a 'baboon drill' so that when the baboons do come

looking for food, everyone from the teachers to the children knows just what to do. The principal, Bevil Velensky, has made understanding baboons an important element of school life, and learners have designed a super website which shows, from their point of view, how to cope with baboons within the school environment.

When the monitor project had run out of funds this year and the baboons were in the village continuously, I was so impressed to see just how well the learners behaved. As the baboons entered the school daily looking for food, there was elevated potential for conflict. But despite baboons walking through packed classrooms on more than one occasion, not one child was injured. The children had been taught to stay calm, to drop any food and move away from it and to leave the baboons alone.

The baboons gained few rewards and started to realise that the school just wasn't for them, while the children realised that baboons are a reality of life that have to be dealt with – and how they choose to deal with them made all the difference.

I take great hope from the way in which Kommetjie Primary School has gone about educating its learners to deal with baboon-related situations. The school seems to have an acceptance that baboons do live here and they make every effort to make this situation safe for all.

If one busy primary school principal can achieve this success with young learners, surely we can all teach our own children and grandchildren how to behave and what to do when baboons are around?

Brett Cole

Chapter Ten

A once-in-a-lifetime experience

As with so many things to do with the baboons, the concept of taking small guided groups to walk with the free-roaming troops of the Cape Peninsula has been fiercely debated. As can be seen from the quotes above, those who have actually participated on the walks have found them to be hugely educational, and even life-changing in some instances.

But some residents of villages affected by baboons feel aggrieved by the notion of visitors enjoying the baboons and feel that by taking these walks we are making the situation worse whilst lining our pockets. It is such a shame that a positive educational experience can be seen in a bad light. Perhaps if everyone understood what we have done and are doing they would be more supportive.

Before I started the walks with baboons as a commercial venture, I spent nearly three years walking with the baboons and working with the monitors. During this time I would spend hours on the mountains, learning the routes and where the baboons would be. I learned their patterns and understood their behaviour so that I could pick up the mood of the troop. From their very expressive facial movements and vocalisations I grew to anticipate what was happening within the troop.

With time, I started to take small groups of residents and friends with me so that I could see what impact the groups would have on the baboons, if any. I was also able to see how far people could walk to see the baboons, what sort of questions they would ask and what impact we would have on the terrain.

During this learning period of almost three years, I determined that the visitors have little or no impact on the baboons – the baboons quickly realise that they get no 'rewards' from the visitors and so they carry on with their business, giving the guests a wonderful opportunity to observe them going about their daily lives.

From the monitors' point of view, the walks do not impact on their work at all. We aim to take the guests to where the baboons are. An ideal walk is along the mountains, away from the villages as this is where the baboons should be and this is the best way to see them. But sometimes the baboons have eluded the monitors and are in the villages. Sometimes they are in the dense unattractive rooikrans thickets. Our guides have had to learn to be every bit as adaptable as the baboons to deal with all the variables that go with this type of work, but the monitors simply concentrate on their work and we go to where they are.

It is on the occasions when the baboons are in a village, or on the edges of a village, that problems arise. A few residents even feel that I have 'arranged' the baboons, coerced the monitors to 'bring the baboons' to the village for my sole benefit. Nothing could be further from the truth.

Our guests do not want to walk around boring suburban streets or stand at a scruffy, disused reservoir, far from it! Quite frankly it can be embarrassing as a South African when we take tours through areas strewn with waste and piles of builders' rubble, not the image I would like foreigners to leave with, I assure you.

If I could influence the baboons and monitors in any way it would be to keep the baboons far from the villages as this means our guests enjoy a more authentic experience, and the residents are happy as the baboons are out of their homes – but the reality is that the walks go to where the baboons are.

Another of the concerns expressed is that we are habituating the animals and thus creating a situation where the baboons are not scared of people any more. I think that this is by far the most illogical of the criticisms levelled at the walks. Baboon Matters has only ever taken people to walk with two very specific troops – the Da Gama Park and Slangkop troops. Yet there are baboons in villages from Simon's Town to Tokai, Pringle Bay to Hermanus, and in villages all over South Africa. It is not physically possible for Baboon Matters to be habituating all those baboons in such diverse areas.

The reality is that the only reason that baboons show an interest in humans is if they have food, or offer food or benefits of some nature. We have attracted baboons into our villages because of the rich rewards our homes offer. We continually invade baboons' space on the mountains with our hikes, mountain bikes and picnic areas. Even the research and study groups have impact as they follow the baboons around. The sad fact is that many baboons, far removed from the troops where we take tours, are not only habituated but have learned and been rewarded for bad behaviour for an extended period of time – long before the walks ever started. It is through the walks and the education the walks allow, that we are hoping to undo some of the damage and regain a balance.

Nick Telford

Nick Telford

Lee Slabber

The best way to understand what the walks are about is to participate in one. These excerpts from a story by Illana Stein convey her experience wonderfully —

Before walking towards them, Jenni gives us the rules: no food on your person, and no touching the animals. These are essential so that the meeting of the two species is as stress-free as possible for all parties.

We scramble up the hillside, through thick fynbos, scratchy and fragrant, to where the baboons are making their way down to a stream for their afternoon drink. We follow them down (with a lot less grace and a lot more noise) and deposit ourselves at a vantage point next to the stream. The baboons are all around us, flinging themselves about with that enviable recklessness along branches of oak and pine trees, some a little too enthusiastically — ending up in the water with a satisfying splash, accompanied by our shouts of laughter.

Jenni is in her element, pointing out each individual by name and personality, and showing us just how many of them carry scars or wounds from their interactions with humans. She explains that unfortunately the monitors knock off at five, so the baboons are hanging out at the stream, waiting for them to leave. Then the troop will take a stroll through the village, or just climb the row of pine trees for the night. But as a work in progress it's an excellent start.

The troop continues to play, eat, fight and drink all around us unperturbed by our presence, habituated as they have become to humans. In fact, while the elders tend to ignore us, the youngsters often leap up onto our vantage point and sit for a few seconds, contemplating us with warm brown eyes. At one point, a young one sat next to me, looked at me thoughtfully and then tumbled off the ledge to continue his play. I was amazed at his fingers — old, wizened, wrinkled and black, with perfect nails — and was overwhelmed at his gentleness, so different to any previous experience or perception I've had of this species. In his eyes I could see an intelligent being, just trying to make his way in a very confusing world — well, we can all relate to that, can't we?

The true eye-opener for me was that while they were not disturbed by us, we weren't disturbed by them either. More, I left with a tremendous feeling of contentment and wellbeing that was incredible — and unexpected. With no reason for conflict, we can sit there, just two primates sharing dappled shade on a sunny, windy afternoon.

Brett Cole

Although we strive to do the best we possibly can to educate both visitors and residents of areas affected by baboons, inevitably there will be a few who abuse the ideal or try in some way to minimise the good.

There have been occasions when I have questioned why we continue to offer the walks. We certainly do not make the pots of money that some claim. The answer is the responses we get from people who have taken a walk with the baboons, their attitude and the overwhelming sense of enlightenment makes it worthwhile. An incident that best sums up the impact of the walks happened on a late afternoon summer walk –

It was a particularly small group of walkers, one of whom was a very garrulous ex-army officer. The baboons were well away from the village and it had been quite a hike to find them, but worth it as we spent the latter part of the afternoon in beautiful fynbos watching the baboons forage. I noticed that the man was becoming quieter and quieter as the afternoon wore on. Finally, a little concerned, I asked him if everything was alright. His reply astonished me. He was quite emotional, he said that while he was in the army they had shot baboons for fun, now seeing the baboons and witnessing their social behaviour, he felt deeply sorry for what he had done. Coming from a 'macho' man, his sincere and heartfelt remorse was all the more profound.

Whether our walks offer a young girl the opportunity to overcome her fear of baboons, or give a retired army officer the chance to apologise for past actions, or simply give a family of foreign visitors the 'experience of a lifetime', without a doubt the walks have a defined and valuable role to fulfil.

Only when we have learned to have a more balanced understanding of each other will the primate species be able to co-exist on this small planet.

Walking the way of the baboon

by Noel Ashton, co-founder of Baboon Matters

Many times I have walked the way of the baboon, and along the journey I have learned much about myself. For how can we spend time with these wonderful animals and not pause to reflect on our shared dance for survival along this path of life.

Many times have I followed a troop, observing a respectful distance but closing the gap by experiencing their lives through the ways of a tracker, and witnessing lives balanced within the environment; of allowing a flow of life to offer and utilize opportunities whilst functioning within cohesive families and groups; how fight or flight mingle seamlessly with groom, play, and feast; where gentle vocalisation can rise to a roar as dominance is challenged, and the subsequent calm after the dust has settled and the troop prepares for the night.

These experiences allow for reflection, for they open windows to another world, and remind us of other lives which share our blue planet home. These are signposts which point to many other species fighting for survival alongside the footfall of man, and offer unique glimpses into the world and survival of another primate which lives in close proximity to *Homo sapiens*, the 'wise man'.

This proximity also enables an often-overlooked opportunity for us to observe ourselves through the eye of the baboon, a distant cousin sharing a common thread through time, enabling a different perspective and objective evaluation of our relationship with each other and the earth.

And if baboons could write, what book would they publish on the ways of mankind, and what would they then decide, beast or blessing?

If you live by the river, you should make friends with the crocodile –
Unknown proverb

The only known planet able to accommodate the rich diversity of species currently inhabiting planet earth, is the one we are on. We have no options other than this. Our impact on this over-worked little planet cannot be debated; how we go forward, however, can.

We all have choices to make as to how we live our lives, how big a carbon footprint we leave, how much positive energy we create. We have choices where to live and how to manage our properties. My sincere hope is that we make choices that encompass greater issues rather than our immediate wants, and start to make small but significant changes that will result in all species being able to co-exist. I do not ask that you all learn to love the baboons as I do, but rather that you learn to live alongside them – in such a way that they stay away from the villages because they know that there is nothing there for them.

The title of the book 'Beast or Blessing' is intentionally provocative in the hope that you will re-consider your view of baboons – after all it is up to you. The baboons will keep doing what baboons do, but you can make changes. You can examine your choices and hopefully through your actions, we will attain a fragile peace amongst primates.

Brett Cole

Tribute

If everyone helps to hold up the sky, then one person does not become tired

African saying

There have been many people who have done so much for baboons and animals, but this year the baboons lost two of the true heroes of baboon conservation. Kate Jago-Davies and Dr Peter Frazer lived in truth and courage and were not afraid to say what they thought and show the world new ways of being with animals. They are admired by all who knew them and sorely missed by the baboons who loved them.

These beautiful words were channelled through Kerry Kronenberg from Joshua Baboon for Peter Frazer – "A true pioneer can never know the outcome or the vastness of his visions – he can only trust and follow them, and allow that vision to unfold. And that is what you did for us, Peter, for all of us – you have given us the space where we can find our similarities and not our differences, where we find our oneness and not our separation. On behalf of all the baboons, our deepest gratitude for your courage, your love, and your dedication to something far bigger than anyone can see."

Who will now care for the animals, for they cannot look after themselves? Are there young men and women who are willing to take on this charge? Who will raise their voices, when mine is carried away on the wind to plead their case? George Adamson

Thanks and acknowledgements

I am always moved to see how many people there are out there who are prepared to get involved and make a difference, and I know from my long years of working on funded projects just how many people you do need to see a project through to a successful conclusion.

So it has been with the Baboon Matters Trust's 'Beast or Blessing'. Mosa Le Roux recognised the potential of the book at concept stage and the donations from the Nussbaum Foundation made this beautiful book and our exciting training programme a reality. We thank Mosa and the Nussbaum Foundation for their faith in our projects.

The book itself must be in line to set some sort of record – everyone said it could not be done in the time frame we had allocated (six weeks from starting writing to getting the book to the printer!) Under normal circumstances it would be impossible – unless you have a star like Belinda Ashton working with you! Belinda has been a saint giving boundless support and guidance; working ridiculous hours and creating what I think is an exceptionally beautiful book.

To my dearest Alison who read my draft writings and whose encouragement kept me going. To Pat, who had to 'suddenly' make space in her hectic work load and who edited in record time. Thank you.

My special thanks to Lynette Johnston who put so much of her energy into gathering the stories.

I would also like to thank all the people who sent their stories, sadly there simply was not enough room to include every story in the book, but we thoroughly enjoyed reading each one.

To the photographers whose exceptional images grace this book and convey so much about baboons – more than words could ever express.

'Beast or Blessing' is an attempt to get people to think about baboons differently, and there are so many people working hard in their own way trying help the baboons. There are many people who give hours of voluntary time on the Baboon Management Team – it can be fraught with tension as we don't all always see eye to eye; but I acknowledge each and everyone of you for the effort you do put into baboon conservation and management.

To the people who have supported the Baboon Matters Trust on an ongoing basis, our deepest thanks – without your support, quite simply we would not be able to do the work that we do.

Our thanks to Adam Murry of the Murry Foundation; Anthony Sedgwick of the Polaris Foundation; Marcel Arzner; and to each person who sends contributions – thank you all.

To Wynter whose love and friendship and glasses of wine are a lifeline. To Nola whose courage and dedication I admire.

To the extended families – Noel, thanks for your ideas and contribution and for getting Baboon Matters going way back when…To the Perrins family – my rock and foundation.

To my own family – to my Mom and Dad – thank you for a 'peach' of a childhood and for your unfailing support in everything I do. I love you.

And finally, to the men in my life – Ian, Chris and Nick – you are my world and you mean the world to me. It is not always easy being married to, or being the sons of, someone as controversial as I have been, but your loyalty and love has been the difference. M6